READ IT TO ME NOW!

Second edition

READ IT TO ME NOW!

Learning at home and at school

SECOND EDITION

Hilary Minns

Open University Press
Buckingham · Philadelphia

Open University Press
Celtic Court
22 Ballmoor
Buckingham
MK18 1XW

and
1900 Frost Road, Suite 101
Bristol, PA 19007, USA

First published by Virago Press Limited 1990
First published in this second edition 1997

A catalogue record of this book is available from the British Library

ISBN   0 335 19761 2 (pb)   0 335 19762 0 (hb)

Library of Congress Cataloging-in-Publication Data
Minns, Hilary.
     Read it to me now! learning at home and at school / Hilary
Minns. — [2nd ed.]
          p.   cm.
     Includes bibliographical references (p. 150) and index.
     ISBN 0-335-19762-0 (hardcover). — ISBN 0-335-19761-2 (pbk.)
     1. Reading—Great Britain—Case studies. 2. Reading—Parent
participation—Great Britain—Case studies. 3. Family literacy
programs—Great Britain—Case studies. I. Title.
LB1050.2.M55 1997
372.4 – dc21   96-47865
                                                              CIP

Copy-editing and typesetting by The Running Head Limited, London and
     Cambridge
Printed in Great Britain by Biddles Ltd, Guildford and King's Lynn

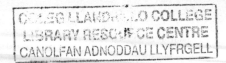

For Margaret Meek Spencer

and with continued thanks to
Anthony, Geeta, Gemma, Gurdeep and Reid

If the culture of the teacher is to become part of the consciousness of the child, then the culture of the child must first be in the consciousness of the teacher.

(Basil Bernstein 1970: 120)

CONTENTS

ACKNOWLEDGEMENTS

My thanks are due to Gemma, Gurdeep, Anthony, Reid and Geeta and to each of their families for giving me their time in 1987 when this original research was undertaken. I also want to thank John Baker, Mr and Mrs Bridle, and to remember the late Bill Thompson and the late Terry McPhilimey who helped me to understand more about the Courthouse Green area as it has developed and changed over the last 70 years. My continued thanks to Angela Webb and Beryl Glasscoe, the children's teachers during their first year in school, who spent time talking to me, and who invited me into their classrooms to observe the children and to 'borrow' them at odd times, and who read and commented on drafts of their reading biographies. Thanks also to my colleagues Sue Davis, Anne Baker and Mike Torbe, who took time to read and comment on original drafts for the first edition of this book, and to Tony Burgess for his advice and support when I carried out the original study. I am grateful to Jane Miller for her encouragement and editorial help in the publication of the first edition, and for her continued support. I would also like to thank Ann Ketch for allowing me to refer to her 'Delicious Alphabet' and Colin Touchin for his insights into the links between the teaching, learning and presentation of musical and literary texts.

I owe a particular debt of gratitude to Margaret Meek Spencer, who encouraged me initially with this project. Over the years her enduring influence has helped teachers all over the world to understand more about the reading process, and in particular to appreciate why children need stories and rhymes in their lives, to read and to grow on. It gives me particular pleasure to dedicate this edition of the book to her.

PREFACE TO THE

SECOND EDITION

Read it to me now! was first published in 1990. The central purpose of that first edition was to document the reading lives of five young children who started school together in 1986, and to examine the range of literacies they learned at home and at school over a period of about ten months. The purpose remains substantially the same in this second edition. The book's main arguments are twofold: first, that reading is a social practice that begins in the home, where children have access to many forms of reading and writing long before they come to school. Secondly, that if teachers and parents can work together to understand these early pathways to literacy, they will be in a better position to develop literacy programmes that are geared to the needs of each individual child and that support children's reading development both in school and beyond.

I am delighted to have been given the opportunity of revising this book because I have been able to reflect on my original evidence and to rewrite parts of the text in order to clarify ideas, incorporate new research, and adapt parts of the text to accommodate new readers, new evidence and new educational considerations. This has been an enjoyable but not an easy task. Disturbingly, I have discovered that the study I thought was complete in 1990 is of course incomplete; the process of revision has required me to look afresh at myself as a learner and a writer, revisiting aspects of my own teaching history and reviewing the past. Reworking this book has made me aware too of how my own language has changed and must necessarily go on changing because I am a language user, and this is what happens to language users. I have even caught myself tinkering with some of the punctuation I used in the first edition. What seemed appropriate then no longer reflects my writing voice. Words and phrases that were right seven years ago are wrong now and I have had to search for others to do greater justice to what I want to say. So I have rearranged sentences and paragraphs to suit my present writing needs and changed tenses to reflect the passing of time – though I decided in the end to retain the present tense for each of the children's stories, because even though the stories are now part of each child's own history, the evidence in them remains constant, and in this sense the children are still four years old. The children, now in their teens, are frozen in time, and I decided that their case studies would not benefit from a new retelling.

In rereading my original text, what I remember most about the period of researching and writing is not the mass of notes and the constant rearrangement of papers and books across floor and desk: instead, it was the human contact with people in the school and community; most particularly, it was the privilege of talking to parents and children in their homes, and of observing children at the point of learning. Gurdeep, Geeta, Reid, Gemma and Anthony are now 13 years old. I visited them briefly in 1989, two years after this enquiry was completed, and my observations of their reading lives are included within each of their stories. I could have gone back to them again to collect more data about their adolescent reading habits; the proposition was tempting. But I resisted it because in the end that is not what this book is about. My task therefore has been both simple and complex; that is, to tell the children's original stories again, almost a decade later, in the context of today's knowledge of the reading process. I trust I have been able to do them justice.

INTRODUCTION

The stories in this book and the reflections on those stories were originally written during the winter and spring of 1986 and 1987. I was interested then, as I am now, in ways that children learn to read and how their views on reading are influenced by the social and cultural traditions they learn inside their family and community. This book is built around the stories of five children, and it documents their reading histories over almost one year, covering the period immediately before they started school, and then following them for two terms in their reception classes. My aim has been to outline patterns of learning in four main areas. These are: family literacy learned in a variety of cultural backgrounds; positive strategies for the teaching and learning of reading in the early years; the role of the experienced adult reader in partnership with a child learner; and, finally, the development of school reading policies that encourage parents and teachers to work together profitably to support children's individual reading development. I have written this book for all those people who have either a personal or professional interest in the reading development of young children – parents, teachers and student teachers, and those who frame policy in schools and centres for continuing professional development. The generalized 'experienced reader' I refer to in Part 2 encompasses all those who have a responsibility for supporting a young child who is learning to read, either at home or at school.

When I began this research in 1986 there was no National Curriculum in place, though change was already in the air and teachers seemed to know that their professional freedoms were about to be challenged. Now, ten years later, the National Curriculum is already into its first revision and the teaching of reading is held in place by a framework of legislation. The present situation is not secure, and calls may follow for the programmes of study for reading to be redefined once again. The teaching of reading remains a subject of debate and controversy, both in parliamentary circles and in the media, even though widely-respected teachers like Margaret Clark inform their readers quite clearly that 'there is only limited evidence that standards are falling in the 1990s, and no convincing evidence that this can be laid at the door of one particular approach to the teaching of reading' (1994: 77). Indeed, the evidence in this book suggests that there is nothing simple about the process of learning to read. For each child, the search for meaning is active and complex and involves using a wide range of experience and knowledge.

When I completed the first edition of this book in 1990, the first National Curriculum for English (1989) had just made its appearance in primary schools, and reading teachers who were interested in the social nature of literacy learning noted with a great deal of satisfaction that the document acknowledged that the culture of the home influenced the reading experiences that young children brought to school with them. Even more importantly, the programmes of study suggested that when links could be forged between home and school, children had more chance of becoming confident language users in a variety of situations. Teachers were reminded that: 'Reading activities should build on the oral language and experiences which pupils bring from home', and that they 'should take account of the important link between home and school, actively encouraging parents to participate and share in their child's reading' (DES 1989: 15). There was welcome acknowledgement, too, in the programmes of study for writing, of the variety of written language that children saw around them at home, sometimes in more than one language, and of its importance for their early literacy development:

> Pupils will have seen different kinds of writing in the home
> – their names on birthday cards or letters, forms, shopping
> lists and so on. Those whose parents are literate in a language other than English may have observed writing in their

own first language, for which there may be a different writing system.

(DES 1989:17)

These statements, enshrined in law, supported our knowledge that children arrive at school having already had access to forms of print, and that each one brings their own unique identity as a language user to school. But this document as a whole failed to quell the growing national concern about literacy learning in our schools and a revised version was introduced in 1995. The programmes of study for reading at Key Stage 1 still contain many statements that reflect considered research and good practice, but I look in vain for those important references to the language and literacy experiences in the home that were so impressive in the earlier document. Yet studies like Denny Taylor's *Family Literacy* (1983) and Shirley Brice Heath's *Ways with Words* (1983) demonstrate conclusively that children's knowledge of literacy begins before they come to school and influences the way they see themselves as readers and learners. It is possible that a further revision of the National Curriculum will remove some of the richness that is there now and teachers will be expected to simplify the process of teaching reading still further, perhaps by overreliance on certain strategies at the expense of others. And of course any programme of study, however well intentioned, can never in itself accommodate the whole process of learning to read. The nature and complexity of this task, and its significance for each individual child, will always ensure that good reading teachers go beyond the text, whatever it may be, and observe and respond to the ways young readers go about the reading task for themselves.

A reading teacher learns

When I was training to be an infant teacher in the 1960s, I was given some guidance on methods of teaching reading that reflected the standard practice of the day. I was shown books from the most popular reading schemes, including *Janet and John* (O'Donnell *et al.* 1949), *The Happy Venture Readers* (Schonell and Serjeant 1958) and *The Ladybird Key Words Reading Scheme* (Murray 1964). I was encouraged to use flashcards to teach word recognition, and told about the importance of having an alphabet chart in the classroom and to direct children's attention to letters and their initial sounds. I was also introduced to a library of excellent children's picture books (the first John Burningham stories were just becoming available) and I was invited to take these picture books into school to read to children. It seems curious now to think that no link was ever made between those delightful and challenging stories and the methods we were expected to use to teach reading. The picture books were entertainment, and reading them to children was something to do at the end of a busy school day, just for relaxation – but it was back to the flashcards and alphabet charts when we did the serious stuff of teaching reading. There was never any suggestion that children might actually read John Burningham's books themselves along-side, or even in place of, the reading primers that occupied the greater part of their reading lives.

Later, with my own class of children, and numerous copies of *Janet and John* primers, I worked hard to teach word recognition and letter-blends as I had been taught to do. I organized my teach-ing time so that I heard every child read as often as I could, some-times growing impatient if they couldn't recall words I felt they should know – it was easy to transfer my burden of anxiety on to their shoulders. I knew no better. Now, when I hear remarks from politicians and members of the aristocracy about so-called 'trendy' teachers of the 1960s, I wonder where they get their evidence from. These teachers, whoever they were, didn't teach in the schools I knew about in the 1960s and 1970s, and they certainly didn't emerge from my training college. Our problem was that we knew so little about the reading process.

My first real anxiety about children's reading development came with the growing realization that the emergent bilingual children in my class could read every word in the basal readers I put into their hands, but had no idea whatever of the *meaning* (not that there was a great deal there to make meaning from). When I moved to another school I made it a professional concern to find out more about how children learned to read, and my classroom work became an exciting voyage of enquiry into the learning that was taking place there. As I bring some children back into focus, snapshots of their reading lives turn themselves into questions. Why did Natasha suddenly begin to read silently one day, just like that? What sounds was she hearing in her head? Why didn't Jamie choose to read, though I knew he could? Why was that particular story so important for David? When would Zoe read something other than Enid Blyton? In the evenings, or at weekends or holiday times, I read books, articles, attended conferences or joined groups of teachers with the same concerns, and ideas were put forward, discussed, taken up, discarded.

I got myself three sets of teachers to help me learn. First, there were the children themselves; I observed them and talked to them, noted their likes and dislikes, their enthusiasms and difficulties, all the time trying to work creatively with them to support their reading development. Secondly, there were teacher-colleagues – people who taught me that there were many ways into reading, who put books like Sylvia Ashton-Warner's *Teacher* (1963) in my hands with its emphasis on real key words to dignify children's own language learning. Crucially, these colleagues persuaded me that the stories I read at the end of the school day could actually be a crucial element in the acquisition of early reading, and not simply an entertaining add-on extra. Finally, my teachers were the authors of books about the teaching and learning of reading. I knew from Frank Smith (1971, 1973, 1978) that I could make the task of learning to read easier for children by helping them to make sense of what they read, rather than always insisting on accuracy. Instead of criticizing, I had a way of learning from errors; I could now celebrate a young reader's inventiveness and creativity, and view 'mistakes' as positive evidence of the vast amount of linguistic knowledge and experience they brought to the task of reading. At the same time, I learned from Margaret Meek and her colleagues who wrote and edited *The Cool Web* (1977) the importance of putting literature at the forefront of children's reading lives.

Looking back on those years as a reading teacher, I realize now that I still wasn't able to answer to my satisfaction many important questions about reading. I know now that although I had tried to see each child as a full person my ideas had been framed solely around the child as individual learner. In other words, I had taken no account of the collaborative manner in which children learn to read and write, even though I saw evidence of it in front of my eyes. I saw no reason to acknowledge the social and cultural contexts in which the children's literacy learning took place because I had not yet discovered that the learning we do is mediated through our negotiation with other people. The world of the children as I perceived it was my world of the classroom, and what was important was what happened there. Of course, I knew the children's parents and spoke to them, sometimes at length, on parents' evenings, but I never paid much attention to the kinds of knowledge and experiences of reading that were part of their lives – not particularly because I wanted to hold myself away from this aspect of the children's experience, but because I had no idea that I ought to be listening to and observing the way these families used reading and writing in their homes. If I had, I would have had a firmer base from which to investigate the children's reading environment and to understand about their own world of experience, their own lived lives.

Some years ago, the responsibility of a headship brought me into a different, less restricted relationship with a new school community. After spending time discovering my own role, getting to know people in school and out, and learning about new sets of community values, my interest in language resurfaced and I wanted to formulate a school reading policy that reflected my concerns about learning to read. Coincidentally, I was urged to read *Ways with Words* by Shirley Brice Heath (1983). This landmark book, with its exciting analysis of language and culture in two communities, gave me a fresh view of reading. An example is in order. Here is Brice Heath describing one of many reading practices she observed in the black working-class community she calls Trackton:

> Reading was a public group affair for almost all members of Trackton from the youngest to the oldest. Miss Lula sometimes read her Bible alone, and Annie Mae would sometimes quietly read magazines she brought home, but to read alone was frowned upon, and individuals who did so were accused of being anti-social. Aunt Berta had a son who as a child used to slip away from the cotton field and read under a tree. He is now a grown man with children, and he has obtained a college degree, but the community still tells tales about his peculiar boyhood habits of wanting to go off and read alone.
>
> (Brice Heath 1983: 191)

The images of these people reading in Trackton have remained with me to this day, along with many others from the book. I had never read observations about reading like these before and they excited me. I knew that if I wanted to learn more about the children and their reading in my own school, I had to get out into the community to begin to make sense of the world the children were living in, and to focus on the ways their families used reading and writing in their own lives. Without this basic understanding I knew it wouldn't be possible for me to learn more about patterns of reading in and out of the classroom. I took up the challenge, and the first edition of this book grew out of the research I did with five families for an MA study completed in 1987.

The teaching of reading: yesterday and today

From the very first day when the five children in this study started school their teachers encouraged them to choose, handle and read books. They helped the children to relate the meaning of stories to their own lives, and to join in or take over the reading if they felt confident enough to do so. They were encouraged to read with older children and with children in their own class, so that from time to time they became each other's reading partners and teachers. Knowledge of letters and initial sounds were taught with reference to the text the child was reading, rather than as isolated chunks of knowledge. This multilayered teaching pattern might seem commonplace today, but it was not always so.

Thirty years ago, when Reid's teacher began teaching at the same school, her head teacher told her that the young children in her class had to know all 26 letters of the alphabet by the end of their first term in school, and should have read the first yellow *Janet and John* primer perfectly by Christmas. In response to this pressure, she stayed behind after school each evening until five o'clock to hear children read. 'Their parents would leave them as long as I could stay', she remembers. Interestingly, this wasn't the way she'd learned to read herself. 'My dad taught me', she says. 'He used to read to me for hours. I nearly always had an adult to read with, grandmother or auntie. I could read before I went to school and I could write a bit as well.' Like many other teachers, she set this experience aside and took on the professional view of teaching reading she had learned at training college, just as I did. Over the years *Janet and John* readers were replaced by other primers, notably *Kathy and Mark Basic Readers* (O'Donnell and Munro 1966) and later *Reading 360: The Ginn Reading Programme* (Britton and Root 1978). The tradition of keeping children at school after hours to read to their teacher had long since ended but for many years children were still encouraged to learn to read using word recognition as the main teaching strategy, and they took word tins home containing new words for their parents to help them learn – this used to be a common practice in infant schools, and was an interesting forerunner of the home–school learning policies that have been in the forefront of educational thinking in community education in Coventry since the 1970s, and which are documented by Widlake and Macleod (1984). Let us pause to look briefly at this method of teaching reading, so reliant on the recognition of individual words and the sounds that make up those words. It is based on behaviourist theories of learning where the reading process is broken down into manageable parts, each to be mastered separately and presented to children in small graduated steps. A. E. Tansley summarizes this approach to managing the teaching of reading:

> A good reading programme consists of four parts: the development of readiness; the acquisition of a sight vocabulary of words which occur frequently in children's reading and spoken vocabulary; the development of independent reading by the use of phonic analysis and synthesis and other word recognition techniques; the development of speedy, relaxed silent reading for content, ideas and pleasure.
>
> (Tansley 1967: 28)

The imposition of this method actually made the process of learning to read more difficult for many children. The overreliance on word accuracy meant that they were denied early access to other kinds of reading knowledge, principally the support of patterned and meaningful texts to help them predict what they were reading and to keep the momentum going. When they were given a book to read its language was often so contrived, its subject matter so minimal, and its illustrations of such poor quality, that it was scarcely worth the trouble of reading. But the situation could hardly have been otherwise given the constraints of this reading methodology. In addition, children were denied access to an emotional response because there was so little in the book to engage with. Is it any wonder that some turned their backs on reading?

In the 1970s there was a significant shift towards the acceptance of psycholinguistic theories of learning. These gained support in schools, and what followed was a gradual move away from total reliance on skills that focused on word accuracy towards other forms of reading knowledge that increased a child's ability to anticipate, join in, and respond to the meaning in a book. These theories were given prominence by reading teachers like Frank Smith, who summarized the reading process like this:

> Children learn to read only by reading. Therefore, the only way to facilitate their learning to read is to make reading easy for them. This means continuously making critical and insightful decisions – not forcing children to read for words when they are, or should be, reading for meaning; not forcing them to slow down when they should speed up; not requiring caution when they should be taking chances; not worry-

ing about speech when the topic is reading; not discouraging
errors.

(Smith 1984: 23)

As the views of Smith and others began to influence the teaching and learning of reading, Margaret Meek's work on the importance of story (1976, 1982) helped to persuade teachers that they
would benefit from looking afresh at the books they gave children
to read.[1] Her work was given practical emphasis by Jill Bennett
(1979) and more recently by Liz Waterland (1988), and teachers
started to introduce the kind of books into the classroom that children could read and respond to by drawing on their own experiences, bringing their intelligence and emotional awareness to the
task.

In the ten years since I first embarked on this study, important
new work has taken our knowledge about literacy learning even
further. Margaret Meek has explored the history and the future of
reading in *On Being Literate* (1991), arguing that developments in
technology call forth new literacies for children to become familiar with. Over the past few years, several writers have drawn our
attention to the ways that children use visual forms of literacy in
their reading lives. The work of Judith Graham (1990), Jane
Doonan (1993) and most recently of Victor Watson and Morag
Styles (1996) has drawn our attention to the nature and extent of
children's visual awareness in their reading lives. Yet, as Watson
and Styles point out (1996: 3), there is no specific mention of children's uses of pictorial literacy within the current programmes of
study for reading. Significant new research by Eve Gregory (1996)
is helping us to understand how the reading process is experienced
by some children. Gregory has brought powerful insights to bear
on the way emergent bilingual children begin to read in a second
language, and I have drawn on her work to give greater insights
into the reading practices of Gurdeep and Geeta, the two emergent
bilingual readers in this study.

The research method

When I was a classroom teacher I came to believe that the kinds of
questions I asked about learning ought to be ones that enabled me
to look at each child as a separate human being. They should be
questions, I thought, that allowed children to retain their human-
ity. I wanted this study to share those same qualities, set within
the context of the school community, and to help me towards an

enriched understanding of the five children's lives in a way that
was celebratory, giving them strength and dignity and allowing me
to feel comfortable and honest in my observations and intuitions. I
had been influenced by the kinds of beliefs about human nature
I met in the writing of George Eliot – who, incidentally, lived in
Nuneaton and then Coventry, just a mile or two from the children's
school, for the first 30 years of her life. In 'Janet's Repentance', first
published in 1858, she wrote:

> surely the only true knowledge of our fellow-man is that
> which enables us to feel with him, – which gives us a fine ear
> for the heart-pulses that are beating under the mere clothes
> of circumstance and opinion. Our subtlest analysis of schools
> and sects must miss the essential truth, unless it be lit up by
> the love that sees in all forms of human thought and work,
> the life and death struggles of separate human beings.
>
> (Eliot 1977: 322)

Initially, I wanted to find a way of working with the whole
school community, but was quickly persuaded that this was going
to have to be a modest study, fitted in somehow around a full-time
job. I had read and enjoyed Brian Jackson's *Starting School* (1979)
and thought there was a possibility of working with six children
and their families as he did, but with my central focus being on the
children's reading development. I wanted to work with children
who between them reflected the ethnic and sociocultural diversity
of the school. In the end I chose two white children, a boy and a
girl called Reid and Gemma; Gurdeep and Geeta were choices
because they were Sikhs and their families formed part of our
largest minority group within the school. I selected Anthony since
he was the only Afro-Caribbean boy to be admitted to the school
that year. (The Afro-Caribbean girl in the study left the country
shortly after I began the research and she is therefore omitted.) I
already knew the parents a little, since they had older children in
the school, and this made my initial contact with them easier. First
of all I asked each family if they would be willing to help me
undertake a study about their child becoming a reader. I told them
I felt that as teachers we needed to know much more about the
kinds of reading children saw around them and joined in with at
home, and that it was becoming increasingly important for us to
understand more about the way parents helped children learn to
read both before they came to school and when they were at
school. I explained that the study would involve me coming to talk
with them on various occasions, and monitoring their child in

school. They agreed to my proposal. I also spoke to the two teachers who would be working with these children over the year, and they agreed to help me too.

At this point I didn't have a set of questions in my head, contrary to normal models of research. Instead, I trusted that questions and hypotheses would emerge as I got deeper into the task of exploring five beginning readers and understanding more about the social and cultural dimensions of the reading process. Looking back, though, I recognize that two basic assumptions lay behind my research into learning to read at home and at school. First, since all five children had been part of a print culture from birth, I guessed they would have seen print around them in some form before they came to school, irrespective of the amount of reading and writing in their homes. Secondly, I knew that each child in the study would already have had to find a way of making sense of the kinds of reading and writing that were part of their home life and that therefore they were already to some extent behaving like readers. I carried these basic insights with me during the period of enquiry, and they reappear in the book, intertwined through the children's stories and the analysis of those stories.

I visited each family on three separate occasions and asked the parents about their child, the kinds of reading and writing activities that happened in the family, and how they spent their time when they went out. Sometimes I saw only the mother, sometimes both parents; sometimes the child was there together with older brothers and sisters, who often joined in the conversations. I recorded the interviews. After the third visit I left a tape recorder with the families and asked the parents to record themselves reading with their child, sharing a book they both liked. Finally, I asked each family to list all the kinds of written material they used and saw around them in their home. (This last request was almost unworkable – though some parents initially attempted to make a list, the task was too daunting, particularly for parents who worked full-time.)

Once in school, I observed the children in class when I could. Occasionally I set aside specific times to visit their classrooms, but more often I went to observe them, or talk with them individually, when I had a spare half-hour or so, and I believe my examples are representative of characteristic interactions over their first few months in school. Sometimes I listened to the children reading and I recorded these sessions (with their permission). I also recorded them reading with their teachers and with their peers and collected samples of their early writing. After school, or at holiday times, I talked with their teachers about the children's progress and visited their parents informally two or three times over the research period to keep in touch with them.

Throughout, I tried to be observer, listener, sharer, interpreter and finally storyteller of events in the lives of these children and their families. I never claimed, though, any kind of neutrality; indeed, my own interests, previous teaching experiences and intuition will already have been apparent in my choice of study and the way I decided to define it. It is there again in the five stories, informing my choice of what I recorded, selected and omitted from the evidence. I recognize too that my position as the children's head teacher placed me as an authority figure in relation to the children and their families and distanced me from them, even though they were seeing me in a different role: that of information-gatherer in their homes, drawing on their unique knowledge and experience. Perhaps too the families took up a dual stance towards me: that of traditional parent, a little awed to have the head teacher call round, and that of the secure possessor of knowledge they knew I found valuable. I enjoyed getting closer to them than I've ever been to other families of children from school – eating with them, watching television, talking and sharing ideas.

By the end of the children's second term in school, I had amassed a great deal of evidence and needed to find a way of presenting it that reflected and illuminated the children's lives and their entrance into reading. Each child's life was uniquely rich and I chose to become their biographer, writing each story as it unfolded in its own way, and asking the parents to read and comment as I went along. By the time each was written I wanted to have five personal histories in front of me. I guessed they would look more like literature than scientific research because, like literature, they dealt with human issues by telling a precise story. Any universal truths would come out of the particularities of each story, as in a novel. What follows then, is a glimpse into the living and reading worlds of these five young children.

The arrangement of the book

Part 1, the first five chapters, contains the reading biographies of Gurdeep, Gemma, Anthony, Geeta and Reid as they set out to become readers. The children were all still inexperienced readers in many ways, with only a minimal understanding of letters and their corresponding sounds and very little knowledge of sight vocabulary; yet in other ways they all had a wide range of reading experiences before they came to school. We meet them first in their homes three months before they come to school, to discover the kinds of reading experiences that were already part of their lives; then we follow them into their classrooms to see them learning to read alongside their teachers. As we observe these children, two things become clear: first, they had all taken their initial steps towards becoming readers before they came to school, either by observing or being included in the reading and writing activities of their home and neighbourhood; secondly, they each had some markedly different reading experiences because their literacy learning had been influenced and supported by the social and cultural traditions of their family.

Part 2 explores the children's stories in relation to theoretical considerations and, more practically, discusses ways that teachers can develop policy and practice in their own schools and classrooms. Chapter 6 builds on the reading behaviours of the five children and shows how young readers in general can be helped to develop positive views of themselves, even though they might still be inexperienced readers in many ways. The chapter explores strategies for supporting young children's knowledge and understanding of the reading process – reading and talking about illustrations, recognizing individual words and initial sounds, memorizing significant events in stories, learning to read critically, developing literary uses of language, learning the conventions of handling a book, using metalanguage to talk about books and about language itself, memorizing phrases of stories and poems. Chapter 7 is about the social and emotional world of play, symbolism and story. It explores the role of story and narrative in children's lives, and discusses how children extend their world of make-believe play into the imaginative story world. The chapter shows how favourite books can be used in classrooms to help children understand about different kinds of reading knowledge and to reflect on the multilayered meanings offered by challenging stories. Chapter 8 explores the delicate one-to-one relationship between the young child reader and the significant adult who shares their reading with them at home or at school. It illustrates a central theme of the book – that ways of sharing stories are culturally learned, and shows how one-to-one reading interactions with an experienced adult crucially affect a young reader's development. Chapter 9 is an interpretation of the way children's learning becomes embedded in social and cultural conventions and the implications this has for teachers, parents and children. In this chapter I suggest that children make the best use of their literacy learning at home and at school when their teachers and parents can work together to share each other's views of literacy and to develop closer partnerships.

The neighbourhood and the school

The north-east of Coventry, where the children's school lies, is an area of about eight square miles, fringed by the M6 motorway and giving way to fields beyond it. The area is bisected by a main road, busy with traffic commuting to and from the motorway and outlying areas, and on either side of this main road are rows of streets of uniform council housing, mainly terraced, with gardens front and rear. Much of this has recently been modernised; families have been provided with indoor lavatories and central heating, and some have opted to buy their council houses. Further into the city the houses are older and form dark blocks of terraces, with no front gardens.

The area has undergone massive changes in the last 70 years. Before the Morris car works and Alfred Herbert Machine Tools brought industrial development to the area on a large scale, much of the north-east was farmland, and small communities of close-knit families lived in villages or scatterings of houses along the main road and beyond, linked by pastoral names that remain today in local districts of Coventry: Courthouse Green, Bell Green, Alderman's Green, Hall Green, Wyken Green, Henley Green, Potters Green. Families eked out a living by working as agricultural labourers on the farms and supplemented their wages by keeping chickens and pigs, while the women took in washing. A few of these families remain in the area, though their animals have long gone, and the washerwoman has been replaced by the washing machine or the local launderette. Every so often there are other reminders of the past: weavers' cottages dating from the eighteenth century and street names like Shuttle Street, Weaver's Walk, and Heddle Grove are testament to the involvement with weaving in the area. But names like Workhouse Lane have been replaced by Proffit Avenue, and stuccoed council houses line each side of the road. A Hindu temple was built on the corner a few years ago, close to where Gemma lives. 'They shouldn't have built it there', a young boy told me: 'They bring all their cars and park them down our road. The boy next door lets their tyres down!' – an indication that racial hostility still exists in the area.

The 1920s and 1930s saw the first real industrial expansion as the Morris and Herbert works brought families into the area. 'You got all your skilled workers this side of town', recalls Bill Thompson, a retired Morris worker. He adds:

> The Morris was known as 'The Mint' and when I was 22 I was getting ten guineas a week. There was money to burn around here. Nobody was out of work. You got more money at the Morris than any other factory in England. When I was 15 I was earning three times as much as my father. It didn't matter what age you was, if you earned it, you had it. The sky was the limit.

Soon most of the farmland was being sold for redevelopment to house the workers and their families. The 1960s were still times of full employment and the north-east of Coventry responded by building more houses, two blocks of high-rise flats and a shopping precinct. Full employment continued a long tradition of immigration – including my own – into the area, attracting people from all over Britain and from the Indian subcontinent and the West Indies. Alfred Herbert's employed Indian men in their foundries while many Afro-Caribbean men worked at the Morris factory; their wives became nurses. Some Asian families bought corner shops in the area or, like Geeta's parents, set up clothing factories or other family-run businesses.

But today those with jobs are the lucky ones, and when I began this study in 1986 it was clear that for many the boom time was already over and industry in Coventry was in decline. Unemployment has brought in its train stress, poverty and unhappiness, and old people who remember the area as it was 70 years ago will tell you that as a consequence standards have fallen. They testify to the plight of the old people – white, Afro-Caribbean and Asian – who live alone in the high-rise flats and are afraid to go out at night. They talk about the increasing muggings, vandalism, graffiti, drug abuse, under-age drinking and theft; they despair of one-parent families and speak longingly of a return to a former lifestyle, where you took your cap off to greet a lady or the parson, and watched respectfully as the Church Lads' Brigade marched through the streets on the first Sunday of each month.

The school, built on former farmland in the 1950s to educate the growing population, is set back from the road. It's a stark, sprawling building, standing flat-roofed and inelegant in grounds of mature trees and playing fields: the caretaker is proud of it and says it is a kind of oasis in a desert of bleak houses. Inside, 15 classrooms lead off from long corridors. Two of these classrooms are for reception children, and it's into these rooms that Gurdeep, Geeta, Gemma, Anthony and Reid will go on their first day at school. We will follow them.

Note
1 Margaret Meek also writes as Margaret Spencer. Her publications under each surname are listed separately in the References.

A NOTE ON

TRANSCRIBING

In making the transcripts I have used the following signs:

''   to indicate the actual text of a book;

. . .   to indicate a pause;

–   to indicate a sudden break in utterance because of interruption;

.   to indicate the end of a sentence (as far as it is possible to judge when transcribing talk);

        words in italics indicate where two people are speaking at the same time.

Part 1

FIVE CHILDREN

1

GURDEEP

It was Gurdeep's first day at school. He was 4 years and 4 months old and his mother had dressed him with care, tying his hair in a topknot that was covered with a small handkerchief. She held his hand as she brought him to the classroom; in her other hand she carried a box containing his sandwiches for dinner time. There was a space picture on the box, with a word in large red capitals emblazoned across. 'Transformers!' Gurdeep read excitedly as he ate his dinner a few weeks later, signalling an early knowledge of a media text.

Gurdeep was greeted by his teacher and shown where to hang his bag and jacket. Above his peg she had printed 'Gurdeep' and she pointed his name out to him – an early reading lesson, his first in school, perhaps. Then he sat down in the classroom with his mother and played with the Lego. Five more 'new' children were similarly greeted. Eight other children who had started school the previous week were already making their way confidently around the room. Normally at this time of the morning before Gurdeep started school he might be getting ready for nursery or, on the mornings he didn't go, playing with his Transformers or cars, or colouring or painting, watching television, or talking in Punjabi with his grandmother. Now, as he looks around the classroom, he might possibly remember some of the things that were there when he visited in July: the goldfish in its tank, the doll's house, the home corner, the carpet, shelves and books, a settee and a small red chair; plants and ornaments to look at and touch. Further round, a table with glue, paste and paints and boxes for junk modelling. On the wall, some children's pictures with 'Look at our pictures' printed below; opposite, a blackboard and a noticeboard with typed notices and timetables pinned up and a shelf with jigsaws. Perhaps these remind Gurdeep of the ones he enjoys doing at home. Certainly in a few weeks he will become expert at making the Ship and the Little Red Hen, sitting crosslegged on the carpet in silent concentration.

The clock showed that it was nearly ten o'clock and Gurdeep's mother got ready to go. He waved to her as she left. He was used to saying goodbye to her for a few hours; she had brought him to the playgroup further up the corridor for the whole of the previous year. Today, though, would be the first time he had eaten his dinner away from her. Gurdeep's mother has the same feelings now as she walks down the corridor as she had four years ago when she brought her daughter Tejinder to school on her first day. There's a sense of pride in bringing her son to school now, meeting his teacher and seeing what will happen in the classroom. She has always been interested in the ways the school will help her children to be educated. Every afternoon from now on when she collects her two children she will ask the teachers, 'Are they behaving?' 'Are they taking an interest?' 'Do they need some help at home?'

I already know Gurdeep quite well, having spent time with his family in the final months before he started school, talking with them in their home over cups of cinnamon tea, eating meals together and once going with them to the Sikh temple. Our discussions and my visits and what I have seen, have enabled me to learn about the range of literacies made available to Gurdeep by his family and community. He has been surrounded by several quite different literacy practices in his home ever since he was a baby. These are embedded in the set of institutions and relations that form his culture: the religious life of his family and community, and the domestic life, work and leisure occupations of those around him. Gurdeep's parents have a conscious desire to prepare him for school and at the same time they want him to understand Sikh culture and beliefs. Gurdeep has been read to since he was very small. When he was a baby 'you'd be reading or writing and he'd be out there sitting in that corner and quickly he would pick it up', says his mother.

As Gurdeep's parents tell me this, I sit opposite them on an easy chair in their lounge. They sit on the settee and we drink tea, all of us tired after a day at work. There is a picture of the Golden Temple at Amritsar on the wall, together with brightly coloured portraits of the Sikh prophets. Gurdeep's father has just finished mowing the lawn and the activity has made his hay fever worse. It's a warm June evening and he has taken off his jacket, shoes and socks. His dark red turban is bound neatly round his head. His wife looks cooler in her shulwar kamiz. Tejinder and Gurdeep are drinking orange juice and colouring pictures at the table; their youngest brother Navdeep is in bed. We talk about work and school, gardening and allergies and then Gurdeep's grandfather comes in. He is white-haired and speaks only a little English, but he smiles and says hello to me. Gurdeep's mother covers her head respectfully as he comes in the room. Later, I am invited to eat with the family and we have a meal of vegetable curry and rice with salad. Tejinder takes her grandfather's meal to him and he eats it sitting on an easy chair at the far end of the room. The children's grandmother sits at the table with the rest of us and occasionally encourages Gurdeep to eat more quickly, sometimes feeding him pieces of chapatti herself.

Gurdeep's mother tells me about her own mother, who lives in London. 'She's a good talker', she says. 'She's a very cheerful person. She tells us the stories about her past when she was a child. She tells me all the stories, really interesting, the way she tells us. She tells us when English people lived in India, then when India had been free how the people kill each other.' She pauses then adds, 'I think we all share our life with each other.' It is through stories like these that Gurdeep's mother and grandmother bind their family together with inherited memories and a shared interpretation of history; Gurdeep listens and becomes part of this cultural tradition. His mother goes on to describe some of the kinship patterns within the family structure:

> We are living with the family together, my husband's parents and his sister and our three little children. We live together and we help each other, so we teach our children to help each other and do all sorts of things for everybody. We teach them from the beginning because we always live together and we're expecting the same thing from them when we get older and they have to live with us and look after us.

In this way Gurdeep hears the story of his own life unfolding. As the eldest son he will one day have to shoulder the heavy responsibilities his father now carries. He learns about his place in the family and in society; he constructs himself through the stories he is told about himself. He has already begun to understand that he has a personal history, unique to him. Part of his life is recorded in his own photograph album and he looks at it every day, seeing himself first as a young baby, then as a toddler, and now as a 4-year-old. As he looks back on his life through his photographs from babyhood onwards he is already able to give himself a picture of his world. Each photograph tells its own story and Gurdeep carefully turns the pages of the album, weaving the images together with enormous linguistic economy into a single narrative:

> When I was in hospital I was a baby . . . there's my mum holding me . . . I had a needle in my arm and then I went out . . . I'm coming out of hospital . . . now I'm going home . . . this is my grandma and mum and my auntie holding me . . . I'm grown up now.

In telling this story Gurdeep becomes the author of his own childhood and the storyteller of his own past, incorporating memory into story and creating not only a personal biography but a story about himself that is social, cultural and historical. For the moment he learns to tell a story about himself that places him comfortably within his traditions, but one day his story might change when he feels the need to insert other events and experiences into his past and perhaps omit others that are no longer significant for him. It is our ability to shape our lives like this that anchors us and gives us a view of ourselves as we are now, as we were when we were children, and as we might be in the future. Leafing through his album, Gurdeep reconstructs some of the key events in his life as they have been told to him, and in so doing learns to make sense of the passing of time from babyhood onwards. Gurdeep celebrates and enjoys his life all over again, every day, giving it renewed meaning and taking sustenance from the telling. The frame around each photograph and the earliest and latest pictures act as boundaries to his life, holding time still for a second, capturing moments. The empty pages stretch ahead. At the moment the cultural and religious expectations of his family and community are in sharp focus; the culture of western society, which he meets on television or when he's out shopping or playing with his toys, will be increasingly in the foreground now he is at school.

Around him at home there are novels written in English, magazines, English and Punjabi newspapers, shopping catalogues and calendars. Gurdeep reads advertisements on television, the writing on cereal boxes and on mugs and the information sheet that tells him the names of his Transformers. According to his mother he is usually the first to pick up birthday cards, wedding invitations and letters that arrive through the letterbox, and these are read aloud to him as they are passed around for everyone to see. He shuffles through his mother's domestic papers when she opens her file, and he is interested in the writing and patterns on coins and notes. He sees his parents writing in Punjabi and English and tries to copy them. When Gurdeep goes into the temple he sees notices above his head in Punjabi and English saying 'Silence please' and signs showing where 'Ladies' shoes' and 'Men's shoes' should be placed:

ਜਨਾਨਾ ਜੁਤੀਆਂ   ਮਰਦਾਨਾ ਜੁਤੀਆਂ

Ladies' shoes   Men's shoes

These notices are not only factual statements about where to put your shoes, they also carry cultural messages about traditions and appropriateness that Gurdeep understands and interacts with when he places his own shoes on the correct shelf. This simple example serves to show that language is not just a system; it is the medium for transmitting the social and cultural life of the community. Gurdeep has been inserted into this from birth. The notices also show how the concept of public print has already been developed in Gurdeep's first language. When he meets notices in school written in English such as 'Please close the door' or 'Put your lunchbox here', he will already be familiar with their cultural appropriateness even though he has yet to learn the particular message they carry.

Every month the family borrows books from the library. Gurdeep's mother chooses detective novels and gardening and cookery books, all written in English. Gurdeep's parents always borrow one book from the library especially for him. 'It pleases him, just getting books', his parents explain, adding: 'He gives the book to us when he wants to listen to the story.' Both parents are concerned that he should not choose a book that is too difficult for him. 'We just look at the book. If it's a hard one, then we tell him that you can't read this and you are too young, then we find another book with a few words, a few sentences or more pictures', they explain, showing how their view of the unfolding reading process influences their choice of book for Gurdeep.

The Guru Granth Saheb, the sacred Sikh text, is about five times the length of the Bible, and it is the visual and spiritual focus at the temple where Gurdeep's family worships each Sunday, sitting cross-legged, heads covered and feet bare, his father on one side of the room and his mother, aunt and the children on the other, facing towards the holy book. Sometimes they talk together or greet other families, and sometimes Gurdeep's mother joins in the singing and prayers. The Guru Granth Saheb, probably the most physically beautiful book that Gurdeep will ever see, lies under a carved wooden canopy; behind the book, facing everybody, the priest sits cross-legged and mediates the holy words to his audience. At night the book is taken to a rest room where it lies on a special bed until three o'clock the following morning, when it is carefully and ritually laid once more on the altar. Gurdeep's family hold in their possession a copy of the Guru Granth Saheb bound in two separate parts. One day Gurdeep's mother showed me all the family's holy books. Before she opened the cabinet where they are kept we washed our hands and Gurdeep's sister chose to cover her head and wash her mouth. Gurdeep's mother reached to the back of the shelves and carefully drew out prayer books and stories of the lives of the Gurus, each covered with gold and purple cloth. Then she showed me a volume of the Guru Granth Saheb, unwrapping the folds of cloth to reveal a large and beautifully bound book. She described how the family read and study the text together:

> Sometimes my mother-in-law reads aloud and we all sit and sometimes I read and they all listen, but sometimes we call other people and have a bit of sermoning. It's like having a small function. We invite people and we borrow a holy book from the temple and the lady sings and we read the hymns together or say the prayers and the music is played by some ladies and then we have a meal afterwards.

At other times Gurdeep sits crosslegged with his mother on the settee while she reads to him from the holy book. 'Gurdeep sits with me and he wants to touch it', his mother explains. 'I tell him the words are in Punjabi.' The holy book emphasizes a life of service and of responsibility to the family and the community. When

Gurdeep is older he will go to the temple school to learn to read and write in Punjabi so that he can read the text of the Guru Granth Saheb for himself. He will come to understand that he has a duty to do useful work, to raise a family, and to take an active part in society; that he should eat a healthy diet, keep himself clean and dress correctly. In his neat dress, his self-discipline and his honesty, Gurdeep brings with him to school some of the high values which his culture and religion expect of him. In this way the Guru Granth Saheb serves as a continuing spiritual teacher and guide for his family. It enables Gurdeep to see his community in control of cultural and literacy practices; the holy book provides the community with a framework for keeping in touch not only with Sikh culture, but with the distant towns and villages of his parents and grandparents: a kind of portable homeland for the Sikh population in Coventry.

In Gurdeep's home, telling or reading stories from India is an important way for the family to maintain their cultural identity and their history. His mother remembers:

> In India when it's really hot weather and we sleep outside, we take the beds out and make them very close to each other. We sit on the beds and grandfather and grandmother used to tell stories. We look at the stars and the birds flying in the evening, then the old person would tell the stories. It's very common in India.

In remembering, her reminiscence is itself a story. Now, when she has time and isn't tired, she tells stories to Gurdeep in Punjabi and her stories serve to remind me that he is the inheritor of a rich oral tradition of storytelling. 'Telling by yourself makes them a bit different,' she says, 'you can add a few things more when you are telling by yourself.' In the telling she maintains the continuity of traditional values that come directly from the oral tradition; her fables remind Gurdeep that there is a right way for him to live his life. Here, then, is one of her moral tales which she tells in English, her second language:

> Once upon a time in a village there was a pond. There lived so many fishes and a tortoise; it's quite a big one. They are all very friendly and there's every day two birds come to eat the fishes. They stand near the pond and talk to the tortoise. They become very friendly.
>
> One year there was no rain. The pond was getting dry and day by day all the fishes were dying without water and one

day both birds were talking and the tortoise heard them saying that there's going to be no rain and the pond is getting dry
and we can't get food here, so we're going to move somewhere else to another pond.

When the tortoise heard the friends talking like that he
was worried also where he was going to because he can't fly,
he can't walk very fast. So he begged the birds to take him
away with them because as they were his friends. The birds
they listened to the tortoise and they start to think how to
take him to another city, or to another country, to another
pond. Then after quite a lot of thinking they decide they'll
have a big stick. They both would hold the big stick in their
mouths and the tortoise have to hold the big stick in the middle so he can fly.

Once they decide, they found a big stick. Both birds were
flying with the big stick and the tortoise was holding in the
middle. And the birds told the tortoise as he was a chatterbox,
'When we are flying with you please don't talk.'

'I won't talk.' Then they started their journey. They're flying. And when they were flying, they were flying over a village and there were some children. They were playing in the
field and one child he saw the birds flying and he told the
others, 'Look, the tortoise fly!' and all the children started to
laugh at the tortoise and they all started to make noise. 'Oh
look, the tortoise is flying!'

When the tortoise heard that he couldn't stop to say anything. He talk. He tried to say something. He opened his
mouth and he fall. He fall hard on the floor and he died.

From this story we have to learn the lesson that don't try
to be a fool when somebody tries to tease you. Think what
you have to say. Think about yourself first, then answer back.

And so at home Gurdeep hears about the foolish tortoise and
learns a little common sense. I know of no stories in school that
Gurdeep has heard that follow the form of the moral tale as closely
as this. At school there are only a few books of fables and most of
the stories in Gurdeep's class belong to the tradition of western
Europe. In fact, the culture of the school largely presents Gurdeep
with a different form of narrative; the fairy tales he enjoys come
from a European tradition. (After several weeks in school *Teeny
Tiny and the Witch Woman* (Walker 1975) was his firm favourite.)
Folk-fairy tales contain their own ethical code and the central
character often learns valuable lessons about the right way to live,

but the formula is different from that of the moral tale or fable because in the end good triumphs and evil is punished. I can only guess how much these two cultural perspectives on narrative have influenced Gurdeep's own stories but certainly the Transformer story he told me during his second term in school catches the flavour of the fairy tale. Gurdeep makes sure that good triumphs and evil gets its just deserts:

> All the baddy evils came to fight and Optimus Prime quickly changed. Then he got his gun. Then he quickly fighted. Then the fight was finished and the baddy ones were all burned . . . and Optimus Prime won again.

One of the stories that Gurdeep grew to like towards the end of his second term in school was a version of *Goldilocks and the Three Bears* (Southgate 1971) and he wanted to listen to this story over and over again. He said that it was his favourite story; interestingly, it does not follow the narrative form of the fairy tale. In fact, in some ways it is more akin to the moral tale – Goldilocks does something wrong and receives her punishment. She is frightened by the bears and scared that her mother will find out where she's been. So there is no happy ending and nothing is resolved. We are not even told if Goldilocks is repentant. Does Gurdeep like this story so much, I wonder, because he can implicitly recognize within it elements from both the fairy tale and the moral tale? He certainly has a rich experience of the narrative form of two cultures. Here, he reads part of the story with his teacher:

Teacher: 'So Goldilocks climbed up on to the very big bed but it was too . . .'
Gurdeep: Lumpy.
Teacher: 'Too lumpy. Then she climbed on to the medium-sized bed but it was too . . .'
Gurdeep: Smooth.
Teacher: Yes. 'Then Goldilocks lay down on the tiny bed. It was just . . .'
Gurdeep: Right.
Teacher: 'And soon she was fast asleep.' There she is lying on the bed.

Gurdeep's teacher lends him the support of a skilled language user while he grows towards an understanding of the text, pausing for him to say the words he knows while she points to them and at the same time, drawing his attention to the meaning through the pictures. When Gurdeep and I share Where the Wild Things Are (Sendak 1970) I pause in the reading to ask him for information that I feel will give him a deeper understanding of Max's motives and fears. His responses shows me that he has a good understanding of the deep meaning of the story:

HM: '. . . and he sailed off through night and day and in and out of weeks and almost over a year to where the wild things are'. Who is he sailing away from?
Gurdeep: From his mother.
HM: Why?
Gurdeep: 'Cos he's very naughty boy.
HM: Why does he want to go away?
Gurdeep: 'Cos he doesn't like her.

At school when Gurdeep reads with an adult the story-reading sessions nearly always follow this interactive pattern of a conversation between teacher and child, and this perhaps seems 'normal'. But at home story reading takes place within a different social and cultural tradition. At night Gurdeep and his sister share a story that is usually read by their father before they go to sleep in their bunk beds. He reads them a book chosen from the library, either written in English or with a dual English and Punjabi text, and chosen to reflect the culture of India 'so that they know their own culture, the background', he explains. 'I stop and ask if there's a hard word I think they might not have understood', he adds. One evening, one of the Indian folk tales he reads is called, perhaps significantly, *The Naughty Mouse* (Stone 1985), the title giving a clear moral lead on how the story is to be read and interpreted. Gurdeep's father introduces the book and begins reading. After the first sentence he pauses to ask if the children have understood the meaning behind the title:

Father: The title of the story is 'The Naughty Mouse'. Right. Listen, children. 'There was once a very naughty and cunning mouse. He was always looking for mischief.' Do you both understand?

They say they do and he continues reading for about three minutes. Halfway through the story he pauses to see if Gurdeep has understood and to share his own observations about the mouse's character:

Father: Cheeky mouse, ain't he?
Gurdeep: Yes, he's a naughty mouse.

Father: He's a naughty mouse.

Gurdeep takes it upon himself to explain why, saying: 'He hits everyone, doesn't he? Therefore he's naughty.' His father then reads to the end of the story without making any further observations. When they reach the end Gurdeep pleads for another story – 'Read this one now! Read this one!' he says excitedly and his father begins *Nanda in India* (Furchgott 1983), the story of a boy living in England who goes to India to visit his grandmother for the first time. Gurdeep hums to himself as he listens to his father read; he and his sister appear to adopt a listening role, as their father initially requested. But halfway through the book when Gurdeep's father has been reading for a few minutes, he comes to a part of the story where Nanda is taken to the market to see the snake charmers. Gurdeep looks at the picture of the snake and when his father turns the page over, Gurdeep suddenly requests him to turn back. The picture of the snake seems to have triggered a memory:

Gurdeep: I want to see the snake again.
Father: Pardon?
Gurdeep: I want to see the snake again.
Father: You want to see the snake again?
Gurdeep: Yeah.
Father: There it is. [He turns back.]
Gurdeep: I went to see it in the cage, in the cage.
Father: Where?
Gurdeep: In the cage. Look!
Sister: Where? Twycross Zoo?
Gurdeep: Yeah. They have to put them . . . put it in the box and you have to get a snake, you don't have to hold it, you have to put it in a small box and put it in paper and close it and put water in there and it can swim.
Father: I don't know what you're talking about. OK. Sit down.
Gurdeep: A snake!
Father: Listen, OK.

Gurdeep's detailed account of something he has seen, perhaps at the zoo or perhaps on television, can't be framed and extended by his father because the two don't share the same background general knowledge, and perhaps also because father and son don't share the same sociocultural knowledge of reading and listening patterns. Although Gurdeep's father is patient and polite he seems uncomfortable when Gurdeep takes control by moving too far from the text and initiating more of a conversation than he can handle. If this is so then there is no way of building a context for Gurdeep's snake story to develop, even when his sister tries to bridge the gap between Gurdeep's experience and his father's perplexity. Gurdeep's father could possibly have responded by telling Gurdeep about snake charmers he had seen, but clearly this could not have felt appropriate for him. There is nothing for it but to continue reading and Gurdeep's father turns to the next page which describes a procession through the Indian village. Gurdeep interjects again when he sees an elephant in the illustration:

Gurdeep: An elephant and a zoo.
Father: It's not a zoo. It's some sort of procession.

Then perhaps sensing Gurdeep's interest he adds:

Father: It's a huge elephant, isn't it?
Gurdeep: Yes.
Father: Very well decorated. Mmm . . . Must carry on.

But Gurdeep wants to talk about the elephants:

Gurdeep: I want an elephant at home that can sit on here and can
            walk. They don't run. They just walk like this . . .
Sister: Slowly.
Father: Mmm. OK.

Once again Gurdeep's father is compelled to return to the text. Why does he feel the need to do this? Possibly he is tired after a day at work; perhaps, too, the effort of sustaining a conversation in English – the second language of all three participants – is too much. And no doubt the tape recorder puts pressure on him to 'perform' to some extent. And I think there may be another reason too and this is to do with the father's own ways of listening to and making sense of texts. He is used to taking the role of listener himself at the temple when the words of the sacred book are mediated to him through the priest, without interruption. He associates the modes of reader and listener, in other words, with the ritual relationship of reader authoritatively mediating texts and listener receiving actively but without interrupting. It might then seem appropriate for his children to behave similarly when he reads to them. So although his responses may appear repressive to some teachers of young children, they are in fact a gift of cultural inheritance to Gurdeep and his sister.

And perhaps Gurdeep is modelling his reading behaviour on his father's when he retells *Where the Wild Things Are* to his classmate

Simon at school. He is interested in sharing the enjoyment of the story with Simon, but clearly wants to hold on to the telling:

Simon: Read the book!
Gurdeep: I can read it.
Simon: Go on then.

I watch from a distance and notice how Gurdeep holds the book confidently, turning each page and 'reading' the illustrations with care. Here is an extract from his retelling:

> Then he's going to kill the dog. Dog . . . ranned away. He went to sleep with no dinner. The bedroom grow . . . grewed and and grewed. It became . . . mother said no . . . ah . . . no I missed the other page [he turns back]. Ah he said mother I'll eat you up. The . . . the . . . garden growed and grewed and growed the . . . his mother said your . . . I called you wild Max. He buyed . . . he buyed a new boat he have to sail right to monsters.

It is perhaps already clear that even though Gurdeep is not reading the text in the conventional way (his eyes are not moving along the line of print) he nevertheless has a strong memory for this text, based on his previous experience of hearing it read aloud. It is possible too that the literary form of the language, with its rhythmic quality, its musicality and its imaginative outpourings, helps Gurdeep to remember some of the phrases and to paraphrase others. He certainly has an overall feel for the 'tune' of the writing, and he can 'hear' where he has not been faithful to the retelling. In the following extract his first attempt at 'out of the water . . .' does not fit his memory of the correct intonational pattern, so he tries again:

> Then . . . he he he went in the private boat that came out of . . . Out of the water came a big monster and he [blows] did that and Max was scared then they went down. Down he went. He said I'm coming out. They gnashed their terrible . . . gnashed they gnashed their terrible . . . ter . . . eyes. Tashed their terrible. Tashed their terrible teeth and tashed terr – showed their terrible claws.

Words like 'private' and 'gnashed' are not in Gurdeep's everyday vocabulary. But he has remembered them and inserted them into this telling, confirming how important it is to read and reread stories to children so that they can hear, remember and extend their language. Gurdeep continues:

Then Max said don't just get off this ground. I'm going to be the king. He danced and he danced . . . and danced and had a fight. Then he said goodbye and they said we'll eat you up. They gnashed their terrible . . .

Gurdeep has been rather possessive about his reading up to now and has kept Simon's interjections to a minimum, but now Simon thinks he's remembered the text better than Gurdeep and he reminds his friend that 'showed their terrible claws' is actually how the text should go. But he is firmly put in his place when Gurdeep insists: 'No, I'm gonna read it.' As Gurdeep makes this retelling of the story into a performance I recall his mother's thoughts about the storytelling process: 'Telling by yourself makes them a bit different. You can add a few things when you are telling by yourself.' Now, Gurdeep uses his own developing skills as a storyteller and as a reader to retell this story for himself and Simon.

As he reconstructs this story we see him doing several important things. First, he is learning to control the pace of his own reading – it is his choice whether he speeds up, slows down, pauses or repeats parts of the story; in other words, he is learning to become autonomous in his reading. Secondly, he uses some of the formal language of the story – 'private boat', 'it became', 'gnashed' – and incorporates this into his own retelling, even though he sometimes gets the words and phrases mixed up. His attempts to recall the tone and rhythm of written language represent the beginnings of a mastery of a new genre. Thirdly, Gurdeep is beginning to learn the conventions of book-reading. He knows how to hold a book, where to open it, how to look from left to right along the page and when to turn over. Fourthly, he knows that there is a relationship between the story and reality and that he can take himself in and out of the book as he wishes: 'mother said no . . . ah . . . no I missed the other page [he turns back]. Ah he said mother . . .'

By the age of 5 Gurdeep already belongs to groups who have introduced him to different literacy practices, some public and some more personal, some in English and some in Punjabi. I have several vivid images of Gurdeep as a reader: sitting crosslegged on his settee at home and leaning against his mother while she reads to him from the holy book; sitting on the carpet at the temple while he hears the Guru Granth Saheb being read to his family and community; attempting to understand the instructions for playing with his Transformers; sitting on the carpet in school with the rest of his class listening to his teacher reading *Goldilocks and the Three Bears*; sitting beside his teacher on the settee in his classroom while she shares a book with him. Becoming a reader in Gurdeep's terms means being open to all these experiences and more too, learning what to value and what to discard, so that he feels part of each reading community he enters.

• • •

Two years later Gurdeep is reading what he calls his first 'hard book'. It is *The Owl who was Afraid of the Dark* (Tomlinson 1968) and his teacher has just read it to the class. Now Gurdeep wants to read it himself. At quiet reading time he prefers to sit at his table with his back to everyone else, in private concentration. He reads for half an hour at a time and often carries on when the reading session is over. Gurdeep visits the library every fortnight and chooses six books. 'It doesn't take him five minutes to choose six', his mother says. Some of those he chooses are picture books – I notice that *Gorilla* (Browne 1983) is among them, though he tells me that he now prefers 'hard books with little words'. His mother makes sure he spends part of each evening reading one of his library books and the book he brings home from school each day, and although he prefers reading to himself, because 'I don't get disturbed,' his mother asks him to read aloud at times because 'we still want to listen to him in case he is pronouncing the words wrong'. His father and older sister occasionally read to him but his mother now has no time to tell him Indian folk tales, 'though I talk to the children about the religious stories of the Gurus and Gurdeep knows the names of the ten Gurus now'. Gurdeep goes to Punjabi classes at the temple on Sundays and reads tales of the Gurus in Punjabi and then in English, and his teacher asks him questions to see if he has understood. He has his own copy of a beginner's alphabet book in Punjabi and is given responsibility at the temple for helping to sort the money.

Transformers no longer feature in Gurdeep's life. Instead his skateboard, his football and his yo-yo are among his most treasured possessions, and he reads the yo-yo instruction sheet to learn new tricks. He has a computer and uses it to write with or to play games on. He likes to write on the word-processor at school because 'your hand doesn't get sore'. Gurdeep watches television a great deal and sings along with the advertisements. His favourite programmes are *Bugs Bunny*, *Cities of Gold*, *Dallas*, *The Lenny Henry Show* and *The Cosby Show*.[1]

Note

1 When Gurdeep was 10 years old I worked with him once again to investigate his reading preferences (see Minns 1993a).

2

GEMMA

Gemma looked serious as she came into school with her mother, and as they went past the playgroup where Gemma had spent the previous year her mother said she felt Gemma's hand holding hers more tightly. She wasn't surprised to find that Gemma was shy and nervous this morning; it had taken her a few weeks to settle into the playgroup a year ago. Gemma cried as her teacher welcomed her, and her mother judged that she ought to go away quietly, since the parting was clearly going to be difficult. She said goodbye to her tearful daughter, promising to collect her at the end of the school day, and guiltily made her way home. Despite her tears, Gemma's mother feels that her daughter, at 4 years and 4 months, is more advanced than she was at that age, and she is convinced that Gemma's playgroup experience has made a difference to her development. She regrets leaving school herself without a good education and wants her three children to do well at school. 'I'd like Gemma to get something,' she says, 'not just go into a factory like I did.'

Gemma lives with her family in a three-bedroomed council house a couple of blocks from school. I learn about her mother's aspirations as we sit in the front room drinking tea. Gemma and her younger sister, Jade, sit on their father's knee, and he holds them tenderly. The television is on quietly, and Gemma and Jade are watching a cartoon. Jamie, their older brother, is out playing.

The dog, Sandy, is barking in the kitchen. She had pups not long ago. There is a music centre in the alcove and ornaments on the shelves above. Some of Jamie's school books lie on the carpet.

I don't see any other books around and Gemma's mother tells me that she has little time to read, though at one time she used to read romances for entertainment. Now, though, with three children to look after, domestic chores take priority. When she was younger she belonged to the library, but she hasn't borrowed books for a long time. She says it's too risky bringing them home; she is afraid that Jade will damage them. She writes an occasional note, perhaps to a friend or relative, 'saying "I'm going to see you on Thursday" or something like that', but she prefers talking to people rather than writing to them. Gemma's father, a welder by trade, was made redundant from the Talbot car plant three years ago, and now has time on his hands. He reads *The Star* or the *Coventry Evening Telegraph* in detail, most days.

I ask if Gemma likes books and her parents tell me they haven't noticed her taking any real interest, though she will occasionally look at Jamie's school books. They have an early memory of her owning some thick cardboard books when she was small and they remember teaching her to say the words 'cats' and 'mice' from one of the books. But they were afraid to give her more books in case she ripped them, or scribbled in them. Gemma has never been told a bedtime story. She and her younger sister go to bed at six-thirty each night, and fall straight to sleep. At her playgroup Gemma sits and listens quietly and unresponsively to stories being read to her: her real interest, her teacher says, seems to be in painting and crayoning. But even though Gemma's parents are not book readers or book collectors there is a respect for literacy in the home and an expectation that Gemma will begin to take an interest in reading when she starts school, and that they will foster this interest at home. Indeed, her mother tells me, 'We'll have to get some more decent books. I'll be reading with her now she's starting school. Now she's old enough to appreciate it.'

One sunny morning in early July, two months before she is to start school, I visit Gemma again in her home and ask her to draw a picture. She is now 4 years and 2 months old, and we sit at the kitchen table while her mother talks to a friend in the front room. Jamie sits with us and watches with interest while she draws (Figure 2.1). 'That's a milk bottle with a lady in it', she tells us. I ask her to write 'milk bottle' and she does so, saying, 'That says "milk bottle".' Then she writes, sawtooth fashion, representations of

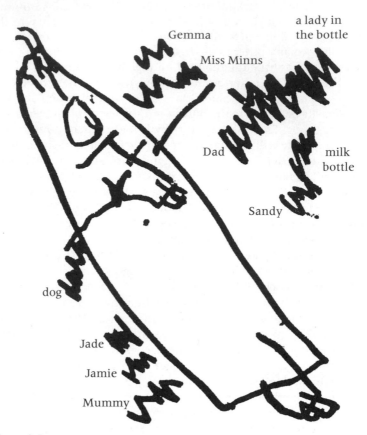

Gemma

a lady in
the bottle

Miss Minns

Dad

milk
bottle

Sandy

dog

Jade

Jamie

Mummy

Figure 2.1

people she knows. Each time she writes, she says: 'That says . . .'
together with the name of the person or animal she is representing
with the marks she makes on paper. There is no doubt that Gemma
has developed an interest in the uses of print and has discovered
for herself the symbolic function of writing. She has learned that
writing is different from drawing, and carries a meaning of its
own. She also knows that writing moves from left to right across
the page (at no time did she try to write in the opposite direction).
At this point in her development she is not able to make a unique
sign for each name, and the meaning of each sawtooth mark is
dependent on the context of her picture and the people she
knows. The number of zigzags she produces for each name varies

according to her perception of the respective sizes of the people represented – see, for instance, her representations of 'Dad' and 'Gemma'.

Where did she begin to learn what writing is? Her mother has certainly noticed that she is starting to pay attention to print in a way she has never done before. I can identify six specific occasions, two from her time in the playgroup, the rest from home, that hint at her growing understanding of the processes of reading and writing. In the playgroup she used to watch her teacher handle story books and listened to stories read to her daily in the year before she came to school. She also watched her teacher write 'Gemma' on each drawing, painting or card she made. At home Gemma's mother has noticed that Gemma watches her father do the crossword in the newspaper. One day she took her own pencil and paper and announced that she was going to do a crossword too. In the supermarket she has begun to pay attention to the food her parents buy, noticing the difference between peas and beans, 'though I think she goes by the colour of the can', says her mother. And she may be right. One day, a few weeks before starting school, Gemma was looking through a drawer and found the birthday cards she had received on her fourth birthday, three months before. 'Is that my name?' she asked her mother, pointing to the printed verse on one of the cards. 'No, that's not your name. That's your name there', her mother explained, pointing it out to her. And a week or so later, after drawing a picture, she asked, 'Mum, will you help me do my name?' Her mother held her own hand over Gemma's and guided her hand as she wrote. It was at this time, too, that Gemma began to show an interest in Jamie's school books. If I had never observed Gemma at home and talked to her parents, I might never have known about her awakening interest in literacy before she started school. Indeed, I might have concluded that since she did not appear to have much interest in stories, did not have books of her own and did not visit the library with her family, she might be slower to take an interest in print than children from homes where literacy was more in evidence. Certainly, the kinds of formal language she will meet in story books at school might appear strange to her.

Today, her first at school, Gemma listens with the other children while their teacher reads a story; and she listens again when her teacher explains that she can choose a book to take home to read. She looks through the books on the shelves and in the library outside the classroom and eventually chooses *I'll Teach My Dog 100*

Words (Frith 1973). This is her first experience of choosing a book to read. At home time, when her mother meets her, Gemma takes the book out of her bag, shows it to her mother, and asks her to read it. This significant act of choosing a book, and asking her mother to read it to her, signals an important development in the relationship between mother and daughter: in partnership with a book. Suddenly, the teacher's invitation to take books home to read and share has made the act of reading a socially significant practice for Gemma and her mother. Gemma is, in fact, bringing the act of sharing and enjoying a book into the household. Her mother observed later: 'Now that she's bringing books home from school she can't wait to bring them in and open them and I say to her, "After tea!" but she wants it there and then. "Read it to me now!" she says.'

It is not easy for Gemma's mother to make this reading time available, and since Gemma and her sister are both in bed by six-thirty, the organization of time becomes a crucial factor. Gemma's mother has to prepare the evening meal, wash up and get the girls ready for bed, and I understand why she says she didn't 'really have time for reading with Gemma' before she came to school. Now, though, she plans the reading time sensibly around her domestic schedule: 'If it's chips for tea, I can sit down, but if I'm doing a dinner I say we'll do it after dinner', she tells me.

There isn't time for reading every evening, and there is no doubt that it's easier to make space for reading at the weekend. Even so, Gemma's mother reads with her daughter with enough frequency for her to observe Gemma's progress: 'She brought a book home with animals in it and she knew every one', she observed. When they are reading together they both focus on the story rather than the meaning of individual words or letters, and they play together at reading in the same way they might do a jigsaw or dress a doll. There is pleasure in the joint effort and they enter imaginatively into the world of the book. For the first time Gemma's mother reads the words of a text aloud and Gemma listens to the texture of written language. Six weeks after starting school, Gemma and her mother read *Me in Puddles* (Wolff 1979) together. Jade listens too, and so three members of the family share this book together – an event that would have been difficult to imagine before Gemma started school. Gemma's mother begins by reading the title of the book, then she reads several pages before pausing and setting up a dialogue for Gemma to respond to:

Mother: 'I make puddles on the floor. There are clean puddles and dirty puddles. I take water from the dirty puddles and put it in the clean puddles. Now I have two dirty puddles.' Ugh! Isn't it dirty?

Gemma: Ugh! . . .

Gemma expresses distaste and her mother continues reading, but Gemma interjects in order to establish the meaning of the text for herself. She comments on the illustration and tries out her own reading of the text:

Mother: 'The birds like puddles too. I am very quiet when I watch them having a splash and a bath. When the big raindrops fall from the dark clouds they drop. Plop. Plop. The raindrops make lots of little –'

Gemma: And the man and that says I am under an umbrella. When the rain stops the umbrella goes on that man.

Gemma and her mother are speaking a new kind of language that they have never before used together. Indeed, the complex literary language in this book is quite poetic in places. The sentence beginning 'When the big raindrops fall from the dark clouds they drop' uses a grammatical construction that is much more common in written than in oral exchanges, and is not apparent in Gemma's everyday conversation with her mother. Interestingly, Gemma has no difficulty in imitating the 'tune' of this phrasing, and echoing it back to her mother, saying: 'When the rain stops the umbrella goes on that man.' Gemma's mother seems to know instinctively that her daughter needs to make sense of the text by commenting on things that happen and matching them to things she knows about in her own life. She stops reading as soon as Gemma interjects and then responds to her daughter's comment, building on it with an explanation:

Mother: Yeah, that's right. Covers him 'cos of the rain.

Gemma: Like you, Mum.

Mother: Yeah.

Gemma is finding her own way of making sense of this story by commenting on the situation and relating it to her own life, and her mother implicitly helps her daughter to construct the meaning of this episode by allowing her to use her own experience to reflect on new ideas, so that the story in the book weaves in and out of Gemma's own personal life. Gemma and her mother use conversational talk to construct the meaning together and to establish the connection between Gemma's first-hand experience and the text. Gemma recalls seeing her mother with an umbrella as she looks at the illustration – 'like you, Mum' – and thus relates this part of the story to something she knows about. Her mother's encouragement shows Gemma that this intellectual effort of matching the text to her real life is a worthwhile thing to do. When Gemma feels she can reread a page on her own, her mother allows her to and Gemma uses her memory of what has just been read to interpret the illustration and construct this reading:

Mother: 'The wind makes ripples on the puddles. I like the splishy splashy sound the water makes, when I'm splashing in the puddles.'

Gemma: I'm splashing in the puddles. I'm walking in the puddles. Splish, splash. That says splish splash. That says I'm walking in the puddles. That says I got my my my boats in the puddles.

Gemma's repetition of 'that says . . .' reminds me powerfully of the way she interpreted her own symbolic sawtooth marks around her milk bottle drawing (Figure 2.1). That same intellectual process of making language mean something is at work here. When they reach the end of the book Gemma's mother asks Gemma to read the story back to her. As Gemma does so, her mother takes responsibility for her daughter's learning by accepting her version of the story and responding positively to the meaning Gemma makes. She makes no attempt to make Gemma read the actual words of the text, so there is never any sense that Gemma will not succeed. This is of central importance to Gemma's whole approach to herself as a learner. Her mother sets her daughter up to behave like a reader, with herself and her younger sister as audience. She allows Gemma to find her own way into the text:

Gemma: That's me in the puddle. I got dirt all over me. When my mummy don't see me I got dirty and all wet. [Actual text: 'Sometimes I creep into a puddle when mummy is very busy and not looking at me.']

Gemma's interpretation shows that she has been attending closely to the meaning. She hesitates before she tries to read the next page and her mother helps her by asking, 'What's he doing there?'

Gemma: I can see myself in the puddle. [Actual text: 'Down in the clean puddles I can see someone who looks like me.']

Gemma gets inside the narrative now. She becomes the 'I' of the story as she fictionalizes herself by moving into the text. When she reads 'I am splashing in the water and walking in the muddy puddles', she is thinking about something she does, or would like to do herself. Gemma's sentence is also extremely literary: 'I can see myself in the puddle' again echoes the language structure of the book. Her normal everyday conversation does not show this formal patterning. As she listens to the 'voice' on the page she begins to talk like the book, taking the structures of the written text and incorporating them into her own reading. This makes her reading powerful, because she is learning to have a new control over her language, reflecting the formal grammar she has heard her mother reading in the story. And there is a feeling of achievement and contentment as the retelling reaches its conclusion:

Mother: You like to move in the muddy puddles, don't you?
Gemma: Yes. No and I likes I likes I fallen down in the puddles.
Mother: Yes.
Gemma: And get all dirty and all wet. So I'm going to bed now. I'll go out tomorrow.
Mother: And play in the puddles.
Gemma: And play in the puddles.
Mother: And get all wet.

Gemma's mother cannot remember how she learned to read as a child, and she has no memories of being read to. Neither of her parents read books, though her father read the newspaper. Yet helping Gemma to learn to read in this way seems as natural to her as helping her to learn to walk or talk. 'I used to read books at one time,' she explains, 'so it just comes naturally.' But there is more to it than this. She is able to respond to what Gemma is doing with a book in a most supportive way – though she is critical of her own flat tones as she reads aloud to Gemma, and wishes she could read as well as Gemma's teacher. She observes sensitively what happens as she and Gemma read together:

When you're reading her stories she takes it all in. 'Cos if I read the book over again to her she's telling me what's coming on the page. In one book she says 'and he told her off' and before I turn the page over she knew it was on the next page.

There are echoes here of her early memories and observations of Gemma learning to walk:

I used to sit at one end and her dad used to sit a bit nearer and I used to say 'Come on', and we used to do it for hours. She wasn't long walking.

And talk:

We'd say everything we'd seen, like. I think 'dog' was quite a quick word with her because she likes dogs. Then 'nan' and 'grandad'. She seemed to pick them up. She more or less learned herself.

Gemma learned to walk and talk with the support of her family. Now, at school, her whole society has widened and she is part of a new social group, subject to new conventions and new ways of using language. She spends time watching in quiet concentration as other children read, do jigsaws or draw, and she joins in when she wants to. Sometimes she chooses not to, and sits on the settee, self-possessed, with her teddy. She is surrounded by print, much more than she has seen around her at home – picture-story books, labels, notices, lists and folders with everyone's name on and she sees children around her reading for themselves in different ways. Some are sharing a book together on the carpet or settee, and others are browsing through a book-box on their own, listening to a taped story, or reading a book with the teacher. Sometimes Gemma chooses to share a book with a friend, and because she has no fear of failure, and trusts herself to learn with help from a teacher – whether that teacher is her mother, her teacher at school, or another child in the class – she asks for assistance when she needs it. Here, she shares a version of *Goldilocks and the Three Bears* (Southgate 1971) with Geeta, who is the same age, and recalls the beginning of the story in her own words as she turns the pages. Though neither child can yet retell everything that happens in the story, they do at least have a good notion of the sequence of happenings:

Gemma: Porridge was too hot and they set off out in the woods. Long time ago. Her name was Goldilocks. Don't know this bit.

'Don't know this bit' means, I think, that she has forgotten what comes next in the narrative, not that she feels she can't read the text. She's trying to recall a story she has heard before, and her memory has been jogged by a picture of the bears leaving the house, and of the porridge on the table. Her 'long time ago' is significant, echoing the language of the tale. Geeta takes over now, and goes back to the beginning as she supports Gemma in telling the story:

> *Geeta:* Once upon a time there was Goldilocks. She came in and she and she's nearly open the door and nobody was there I got that book.

Geeta does not move the narrative forward, but she does focus it in a slightly different way, concentrating on Goldilocks entering the house. Gemma now has the confidence to continue:

> *Gemma:* Too sweet said Goldilocks. Daddy bear . . . too hot. Tries mummy bear. Too lumpy. Tries mummy bear . . . tries baby bear . . . the best, so baby bear now just right. So she ate it all up. Don't know it.

She has remembered the formula of this story, shaped by its pattern of repetition, and now needs support again in the telling. Once more Geeta takes over, and she carries the tale forward with: 'She she sitting in baby chair and she crashed. Really sorry. She sitting . . .' Gemma's memory is suddenly jogged again and she carries on for a while before Geeta again takes over:

> *Gemma:* I know it. She went upstairs and she tries daddy's bed. Too high. Tried mummy's bed. Too high. Tried mummy's bed. Too . . .
> *Geeta:* Lumpy.
> *Gemma:* Lumpy. Tries baby bear's bed. Just right.

Gemma seemed to know that 'high' would not do for the description of mummy bear's bed and she struggled to find the most appropriate word. Geeta told her – the bed was 'lumpy' – and Gemma accepted her suggestion. So it was that these two young girls made learning happen for each other as they constructed the story together, learning how to learn from each other in a context made possible for them by their teacher. They were free to retell the story at their own pace, to take control of their learning and to 'play' at being readers – a kind of rehearsal for when they will read independently. Neither child could have produced this retelling independently and Gemma and Geeta clearly benefit from being an audience for each other and jointly creating the meaning of the story. The nature of this kind of learning can surely be regarded as an important resource for the teacher, who can set up an environment for reading and play where collaboration of this kind can happen.

When Gemma had been in school for ten weeks, she took another important step in her development as a reader and writer. Supported by her teacher, she became the author of a book. Gemma had listened to her teacher read *Burglar Bill* (Ahlberg and Ahlberg 1977) and then she drew a burglar. Sensing her interest, her teacher asked her if she wanted to make her own Burglar Bill book. She said she did, and her teacher made a small book for her. Gemma dictated, and her teacher wrote: 'The big burglar. The burglars. The little burglar. The little burglar stole a pencil. The big burglar stole a rubber. The policeman hurt the burglars' (Figure 2.2). Gemma illustrated her book, then read it to her teacher. The significance of her achievement is twofold: first, there is a sense of celebration. When her teacher put the finished book in Gemma's hand it was a way of reflecting her success as a writer back to her. Now, the story is hers to read and to share. Secondly, and more generally,

Figure 2.2   Gemma dictated and her teacher wrote . . .

she is being encouraged by a sensitive teacher to discover how to read and write in the same supportive way her parents helped her to walk and talk: with the expectation of success. Some time after this Gemma showed me a book she had made for her younger sister, Jade. She called it 'The Burglars'. As she showed me the illustrations she told me the story: 'The burglar puts the things in a bag. The big burglar took the clothes. The policeman got the burglars. The big burglar was sad' (Figure 2.3).

The writing on the first page, ⋂ ⋂○, stands for 'the burglars' and clearly shows the two Ms from Gemma's name. I recall that Gemma was already differentiating between drawing and writing before she came to school, and now she is beginning to pay attention to the letters that make up conventional writing, using those predominantly from her own name to say precisely what she wants them to say in the context of the illustration.

Book-making continues to be important to Gemma: in March, her seventh month in school, this activity was extended by Serena, a 9-year-old in one of the upper school classes who came to work with a younger child in a paired learning situation. She wrote quickly as Gemma dictated this book to her: 'This is my mum. I like my mum. My mum has yellow hair. My mum likes me. My mum takes me to the park. My mum pushes me on the swing. My mum can wash the pots' (Figure 2.4). Then Gemma illustrated her book. It has the quality of a book written and produced at great speed, in response to Gemma's excitement. Serena said afterwards, 'Gemma put all the ideas into it. It was nothing really from me. She likes her family. She thinks about them all the time. She puts them in her stories.' Using this book as a model, Gemma went on to make a book by herself for Jade and her mother (Figure 2.5), using some of the sentences about her mother that she had dictated to Serena. Although she is only really confident about writing a few characters from the alphabet, she has been able to vary their use to make some sentences.

Gemma arrived at school with an emergent literacy of her own, and the classroom context is helping her to develop this, encouraging her growing identity as a reader and writer. Part of Gemma's early success can be attributed to the way her teacher has set up a comfortable context in the classroom, building on the skills she already had when she arrived at school, fostering her delight in language, and encouraging her enjoyment of stories. Gemma is learning about the formal literary language of well-written story books and about the excitement of authoring books of her own.

The Burglars

The burglar puts the things in a bag.

The big burglar took the clothes.

The policeman got the burglars.

The big burglar was sad.

Figure 2.3　A burglar book for Jade

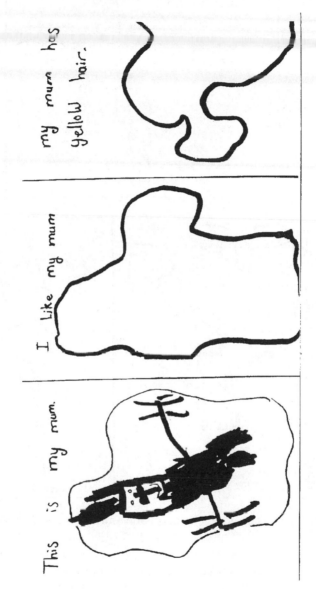

Figure 2.4 Part of a story Serena wrote and Gemma dictated . . . .

This is my mum.

I like my mum.   My mum has yellow hair.

Figure 2.5   Part of the book for Jade and Mum

But perhaps above all she is learning about her own relationship with books and about herself as a reader and writer, appearing poised and confident as she enters into a very special learning partnership with those around her.

• • •

Two years later Gemma tells me proudly that she can now read
Teddy Bear Postman (Worthington and Worthington 1981). She
opens the book with confidence and her eyes turn directly to the
print. Her teacher is pleased that Gemma 'knows what reading's all
about', and though she still needs support, 'I don't think she'll be
long before she reads on her own.' Gemma's favourite stories, she
says, are *Are You My Mother?* (Eastman 1960) and *Dogger* (Hughes
1977). It's clear that her personal and her learning relationship
with her mother are close and intertwined. Gemma tells her
mother about things she's done at school and enjoys reading at
home with her mother who says, 'I think she's done well. For her
age. I'm pleased.' Gemma asks her mother for paper 'all the time'
and spends a lot of time writing. She also asks her mother for help
spelling words and does sums which she asks her mother to mark.
Gemma is far more confident though she still needs reassurance at
times; she is hesitant about writing and needs to know that each
word is correct before she commits it to paper. Her younger sister
Jade is at school now and she sometimes comes into Gemma's
classroom to share a book at reading time and they sometimes
write together.

Gemma is very interested in offers on cereal packets. Her
favourite television programmes are *Home and Away* and *Neighbours* – she has a picture of Jason from *Neighbours* on her bedroom
wall. She also likes cartoons and films on video. Gemma often
helps her mother and offers to go shopping, or to tidy up, or dry the
pots.

3

ANTHONY

The people in Anthony's household, his mother and older sister Paulette, both read and write for their own purposes and pleasure, so it isn't really surprising that Anthony shares their delight in stories and wants to gain a mastery over reading and writing for himself. And since his mother and Paulette have both set themselves up to be his teachers, there is a good chance that Anthony's interest in literacy will be carried back and forth between home and school.

Anthony came along to his classroom quite confidently on his first day at school. His mother, a nursing auxiliary, had arranged to be on leave so she could bring him and see he settled down happily. She had no real fears that he would find his first day at school unsettling as he'd already had the experience of attending two nurseries and a playgroup, and of being cared for by a childminder while she worked, so he was used to being with different adults and children and learning to play in new surroundings. Paulette had also told him that she had begun her school life in this same room four years before and this perhaps gave him some feeling of security.

As Anthony and his mother look around his new classroom they can see a large half-timbered playhouse, a carpeted area where the children can read, or play with the bricks or train set, and share news and listen to stories. There are rows of shelves containing games, jigsaws and Lego sets, and a trolley for brushes and paints, glue and paste. Books for the children to read are stored in red plastic boxes on the tables and there are more books on the shelves near the carpet. Anthony and his mother look at the children's paintings and pictures that his teacher has put on the wall and then, with a last reminder about eating all his dinner up, she leaves him playing contentedly with the toys.

The two children live with their mother in a terraced 1930s house near the school, in a quiet road where some of Anthony's classmates also live. We sit in comfortable chairs at one end of the lounge and Paulette listens to our conversation and sometimes joins in. Anthony is watching television. There is a dining table at the far end of the room, where the family eats together at weekends and leading off to the right is the kitchen. Anthony, Paulette and their mother form a close-knit family group. 'I'd like them to be around me all the time', says their mother. She says they are company for her and for each other when she has to be away from them. She feels strongly that families belong together, especially since her own parents came to live in England and left her angry and resentful to be brought up by an auntie and grandfather in Barbados. Her time with her own two children is strictly rationed however, since she has to work long hours, often leaving home at six-thirty in the morning and not returning until eight-thirty in the evening. Her compensation for working this long shift is that she works just seven days each fortnight and the remainder of the time is her own, to be spent with the children and to organize her household.

Her own schooling in Barbados was much more formal than Anthony's is likely to be, and she remembers being taught to read by learning 'the ABC from a blackboard'. She has memories too of her auntie and grandfather reading the Bible aloud and of possessing a Bible of her own. Church attendance on Sunday was obligatory and seemed to last 'nearly all day'. She recalls that 'everyone took a turn reading the Bible, including the children. Every child had a Bible and children were expected to learn verses by heart then stand at the altar and recite.' Anthony's mother came to England when she was 11 and lived in London before coming to Coventry as a teenager. She remembers reading quite a lot when she lived in London, 'but now I don't read'. Recently a friend lent her Alice Walker's *The Color Purple'* (1983) but 'I just put the book down 'cos I couldn't get time to read it', she explains. She likes poetry and there is a framed poem on the wall, the words appearing below a photograph of two gulls flying off into the blue sky.

Sometimes Anthony's mother takes a book to work to read in her breaks, 'but you never seem to get time, so I just don't bother'. At home she occasionally reads the *Daily Mirror* and *Roots*, a monthly magazine for a black readership. Her cousin sends her *The Nation*, a newspaper from Barbados, and she enjoys reading that because 'I like to know what's going on at home.' On the living-room wall, above the gas fire, are two bright paintings of street scenes in Barbados, and she can recognize the shops portrayed and remember buying things from them. Paulette has visited the island with her godmother, but Anthony must wait until he is older. One piece of writing that made a great impression on Anthony's mother was a project she wrote on Barbados while she was at secondary school in Coventry. 'It's the whole story from Christopher Columbus days', she says; she's saving it for Paulette to read when she is older. Once she tried to write her own life story but became 'embarrassed' as she wrote and, perhaps to avoid facing difficult feelings, she 'stopped in the end'. She doesn't write much now, although sometimes she sits down and writes poems. 'I always have done', she says. 'I get spates where I stop but I like writing. Like last night I tried to think of writing something. I couldn't, so I packed it up. I've got to be in a good mood to sort of write.' She does write to people occasionally but says, 'I'm not a great writer of letters.' She writes shopping lists regularly. Clearly, Anthony's mother has identified her own needs as a reader and writer, even though these needs are frustrated by lack of time; she certainly knows the power of writing, and sees the value of literacy as a way of enhancing her own life. It is not surprising, therefore, that she is supportive of Anthony and Paulette as they learn to become readers and writers themselves.

Anthony has few books of his own and the family doesn't use the public library, but occasionally when time permits all three of them sit down and Anthony's mother reads one of Paulette's Brer Rabbit stories, one of a series kept safely in her wardrobe. Most of Anthony's books are the ones Paulette had when she was small. 'I don't see the point in buying another lot of books', says his mother, with practical good sense. 'He can use them.' Anthony has the taped story of *One Hundred and One Dalmatians* (Smith 1956) and his mother says he knows it well, though she feels he has 'just memorized it'. He likes nursery rhymes too, and the jingles from advertisements on television: 'When they come on he knows exactly what they're going to say', his mother observes. He appreciates jokes too and though he doesn't always get them right he demonstrates a growing awareness of control over language:

Anthony: Mum, do you want me to tell you a joke about the butter?
Mum: What is it?
Anthony: You can't spread it 'cos it might melt.

Anthony has his own bedroom, but never uses it. Instead, he prefers to tuck himself into bed with Paulette, 'but everything is there ready for him when he's decided, "That is my room"', says his mum. All his clothes are in his room, his wardrobe and his chest of drawers. At night, side by side in bed, it's Paulette who shares a bedtime story with Anthony or reads him a version of the Pied Piper or Tom Thumb, or an alphabet book that belonged to her when she was his age. Sometimes Paulette reads his favourite story, one of his three versions of the story of Little Red Riding Hood. At other times she takes a pencil and paper and shows him how to write.

Anthony's implicit knowledge of different uses of reading and writing is already there before he comes to school. He has seen story books and poetry read for pleasure and knows that books are to be valued and cared for, handed down and grown into, like good clothes with plenty of wear left in them. He sees newspapers read and commented upon, and he watches Paulette and his mother write for different purposes. Anthony sees titles of his favourite television programmes, looks at advertisements on television, and reads food labels. The only time the three of them sit down as a family to watch television is when *EastEnders* is on, but Anthony and Paulette watch Children's ITV every evening after school: Anthony particularly likes *He-Man, She-Ra, Knight Rider, Street-hawk, The A-Team, Airwolf* and any cartoons. He can read the names of breakfast cereals and recognizes Cocopops and Weetabix as his two favourites. The family normally goes shopping together, and it's Anthony's job to put everything in the basket.

Paulette and her mother are nevertheless worried about Anthony's attitude to learning. 'I keep on telling him, "You've got to go to school in September", and he's still running about in the garden', Paulette says despairingly. Her mother agrees. 'I hope he pulls himself together,' she says and adds, 'I think school will change him a lot.' She has given careful thought to the way she brings her children up and has clear views on how they learn. She recalls how Anthony learned to talk:

I just let it come on its own 'cos it's better that way. They sort
of pick up things here and there. If you push them too much

it takes longer. They lose interest in what you're trying to tell them.

She has her own preferred way of sharing a book with Anthony and stresses how important it is that he shows he has understood the story. When they are together with a book she reads the story through to Anthony first of all 'so he gets the whole sort of picture of it' and then 'we go back through the book and I say to him, "What's happening there", then he can tell me everything that's happening, before it's happened'. Anthony is receiving important lessons from his mother on how to read and make sense of a story, and about the importance of anticipating what comes next. He seems to know implicitly that as a listener he is actively involved in making sense of the words on the page, with his mother as a guide. He knows too that the illustrations can help him understand the story more fully, and is already skilled at matching meanings across words and pictures. 'You can't just read to him,' his mother explains, 'you've got to hold the book so he can see the pictures.' It is of note that Anthony's mother prefers to hold the book for him (perhaps her own reading teachers held the books for her when she was a child). Anthony will probably need to gain experience of handling a book himself, and of making his own decisions about page-turning.

Anthony's best-loved story is the traditional tale of Little Red Riding Hood. Somehow he has managed to acquire three versions of the tale, and he knows parts of each by heart. He asks for the story to be read to him over and over again; it's clearly very powerful for him in some way. One evening his mother read him one of his three published versions of *Little Red Riding Hood* (Southgate 1972). Her reading took about seven minutes, and she paused once midway through the book to ask Anthony some questions. Then she read to the end, drawing out the literary structure of the text to enhance Little Red Riding Hood's contrition:

Mother: 'Little Red Riding Hood's father took her by the hand and led her thankfully back to her mother, and how happy she was that things had turned out so well. "As long as I live," said Little Red Riding Hood, "I shall never leave the forest path when you have warned me not to do so."'

At the end of the reading Anthony's mother asks him a question which is designed to see if he has understood Red Riding Hood's error of judgement:

Mother: So what did she do wrong?
Anthony: Met a bad wolf.

Then she rehearses with him the part the wolf played in the unfortunate events:

Mother: Yes, what did the wolf do?
Anthony: Ate her up.
Mother: And what did the wolf do to Grandmother?
Anthony: He ate her up too.

Anthony is not sure about the answer to the next question, perhaps because of the way it is phrased, so his mother rewords it, making the sense clearer for him by giving him a strong clue:

Mother: Yeah. And who saved them both?
Anthony: Erm . . .
Mother: Whose father saved them?
Anthony: Little Red Riding Hood's.

Anthony's mother signals that they are nearing the end of the story by giving an evaluative comment on it and inventing a future for the participants:

Mother: Yes. Very good, isn't it? He saved them and they're still
         alive now, aren't they?
Anthony: Yeah.

She gives Anthony the satisfaction of bringing the evil in the forest to an end:

Mother: And what happened to the wolf?
Anthony: Dead!

These questions are designed to check Anthony's understanding of the story. In asking them, his mother is implicitly telling him that the book carries meaning and this is what he should be attending to. The time Anthony's mother is prepared to set aside for this shared reading session shows him how much she values him as a learner, and he knows this. This story-reading session, including the questioning, was approximately 12 minutes long, probably much longer than any other conversation time between mother and son. During the session, and others like it, he learns from his mother that books are important and enjoyable things to give his attention to. He also learns that comprehension is important and that there is a new language in books, a literary language that he does not meet in his everyday conversations. Phrases like 'led her thankfully back to her mother', 'how happy she was' and 'when you have warned me not to do so', set the reading session apart from his ordinary everyday conversations and give Anthony a feel for the language of books.

I know the story of Little Red Riding Hood is deep inside him when he dictates his own version a few months later:

> Once upon a time there was Little Red Riding Hood. She went into the woods and she met a big bad wolf. And he hurried on to the woods. He got there just in time. He pulled the latch and came in. She saw the door wide open. She went upstairs and said 'Grandmother, what big eyes you have', said Little Red Riding Hood and the bad wolf struggled out of bed and gobbled her up in one mouthful. And her daddy came to see Grandmother but it was the bad wolf. He seen a black thing popped out and that was Little Red Riding Hood's grandmother. He chopped him up.

There is no doubt that Anthony is a sophisticated narrator. His spoken version of the story has, in parts, the feel of the language of the book: 'he hurried on to the woods', 'he pulled the latch', 'the bad wolf struggled out of bed and gobbled her up in one mouthful'. This use of literary language was something he already knew about when he came to school. The experience of being read to by his mother and sister and by nursery teachers, and the stories he has watched on television, have all helped him to learn more about how to handle narrative, both as listener and as teller.

At school his teacher notes that Anthony enjoys making up fictional worlds for himself and his friend through play. Three weeks after starting school he and his friend Mark sit at a table playing with Lego. They are making Transformers with the pieces:

Anthony: Mine can change into something else. These couldn't fight us 'cos they were goodies and they could fly

Mark: They have to go up, don't they?

Anthony: [takes wheels] Pretend these batter us . . . mine's bashed up.

Mark: Mine still ain't broken.

Anthony: I'm coming to transform you.

Mark: I'm dead now [throws Lego to the floor].

Anthony: You don't fall 'cos I go faster. You can't still kill me.

Mark: This is your last chance. The wheels killed me once but they can't kill me twice.

Anthony and Mark keep up this intense running commentary to support their game for 15 minutes, planning and creating this fictional world with an ongoing narrative. They are clearly very good at using language to play 'Let's pretend', weaving their fantasy world around their Lego. Anthony's teacher also says he seems to enjoy listening to stories and poems with the rest of the class but never picks up a book to look at by himself, even when invited to and even though he can see other children do this. Perhaps this is because he is read to a lot at home and still has little experience of handling books by himself. He certainly seems to need someone with him while he reads, someone to help create and sustain that story world inside the book. At the same time he does seem to enjoy and learn from shared book-reading sessions with his teacher. Here, he and Reid look through a poetry book with her and decide to read a poem called 'The Toaster' from *Tiny Tim: Verses for Children* (Smith 1981). This poem has the quality of a modern riddle, and the boys have listened to their teacher read it aloud several times to the class. Anthony can recall a little of the poetic language even before his teacher begins reading now. As he looks at the illustration he says: 'with jaws flaming . . .' His teacher affirms that he is right and then begins to read the poem. Anthony echoes her reading and both children join in when they feel confident:

Teacher: Yes, 'A silver-*scaled dragon'*
Anthony: *scaled dragon*
Teacher: 'with *jaws flaming red'*
Anthony: *jaws flaming red*
Teacher: 'sits at my *elbow'*
Anthony: *elbow*
Reid: *elbow*
Teacher: 'and'
Anthony: toasted my *bread*
Reid: *bread*
Teacher: 'I *hand him fat slices'*
Anthony: *hand him fat slices*
Reid: *slices*

Perhaps Reid's paraphrasing of the next line prompts Anthony to enjoy guessing what the silver-scaled dragon is all over again:

Reid: One by one when they done he handed them back . . .
Anthony: A pop-up toaster!

He knows this already, of course, because his teacher has read and discussed the poem with the class before, but there is a sense of satisfaction nevertheless in guessing correctly all over again, and in knowing that he is right. Anthony's teacher celebrates this with him, and makes a game of his reading for him, as she confirms: 'That's right. It is a pop-up toaster, isn't it?'

When Anthony and Reid share *Mr Gumpy's Outing* (Burningham 1970) with their teacher, they are again on familiar territory because she has already read it to the class several times. In spite of this, the questions Anthony asks his teacher are those of an inexperienced reader still learning to find his way around a story book, and I recall that his mother has always held the book while they read together, showing him the illustrations on request. As they look at the title page, Anthony asks:

Anthony: Is this the beginning?
Teacher: No. That tells us the title, look, 'Mr Gumpy's Outing'. And that's the name of the man who wrote it. John Burningham.
Anthony: Is this the end? [pointing to the next page with no words written on]
Teacher: No. We have to turn over another page to find the beginning.

And so Anthony receives some reading lessons from his teacher about how a book works, and about the concept of authorship. She has shown him what a title is, she has told him that the book has been written by a person, John Burningham, and pointed out where the author's name appears on the page. Then she explains that they will have to turn over to find 'the beginning'. Anthony watches as she turns the page:

Teacher: 'Mr Gumpy owned a boat and his house was by a river'. Would you like to live in a house like Mr Gumpy?
Reid: That?
Teacher: Mmm. By the river?
Reid: No.
Teacher: Wouldn't you? Why not?
Anthony: Too many animals might jump around and I might fall in the river and I can't swim.

Anthony has heard this story before and he knows what the central event is. His explanation that he 'might fall in the river and I can't swim' shows him placing himself at the centre of the fiction, merging with the character of the children in the story, anticipating their plight as if it were his own, and perhaps indicating his own fear of water. His teacher's question has given him the chance to build this framework for understanding the story and to explain why it might not be a good idea for him to live by a river. Later on in the story Anthony shows that he knows the text well enough to take over the reading from his teacher:

Teacher: 'May I join you, Mr Gumpy? said the *goat'*
Anthony: *goat.* But don't kick.

His teacher supports him by telling him he is right. Anthony enjoys predicting what will happen next:

Teacher: That's right. He mustn't kick.
Anthony: He's going to kick.

Anthony's story-reading sessions with his teacher present him with a somewhat different experience from those offered by his mother. At home it is his mother who reads and remakes the story through her careful questioning. At school Anthony is expected to take a greater part in developing the story through ongoing conversation. It would be wrong, though, to imagine that at home he is simply a passive listener when his mother reads to him. He is all the time making meaning for himself, and his mother makes sure he attends to those meanings through her questions. This experience has made it possible for him to respond to stories at school by using his judgement and reasoning. Next, he discusses the final part of the book with Reid and his teacher and together they build a shared meaning for the text. At one point Anthony demonstrates how he uses his knowledge of universal morals and values to assess Mr Gumpy's actions:

Teacher: 'and into the water they fell.'
Anthony: Splash!
Reid: Splash went the boat.
Anthony: It was a big boat that was. He shouldn't have let them in.
Teacher: I hope they could all swim.
Anthony: I think so.
Reid: The cat won't be able to.
Teacher: Won't it?
Reid: No.
Anthony: Cats can't swim.

Not only does Anthony use his feelings and judgements about characters – 'he shouldn't have let them in' – he is also learning to make sense of the meaning contained in the book by relating it to his knowledge of the world. 'Cats can't swim', he says; in making this firm statement he moves from the single incident in the book to a generalization about all the cats in the world. His knowledge about cats may be questionable, but that is not at issue here. What is important is that he has justified Reid's comment, 'the cat won't be able to', by taking an intellectual leap from the particular to the general. He anticipates what might happen to the cat in the story world by relating the event to his knowledge of cats in the real world. In this act we see his growing understanding of the concept of causality. Learning to read for Anthony is not only about developing a new way of understanding texts, it is also becoming a means for him to develop abstract thought processes.

Anthony was already an experienced narrator when he came to school, and this is demonstrated in his reading of *The Elephant and the Bad Baby* (Vipont 1969) four weeks after he started school. He uses his knowledge of narrative form, his memory of the language of the story and the cues from the illustrations to guide him through his own version of the story, which has already been read to him by his teacher. The strong rhythm and repetition in the text make this an ideal picture book to help Anthony learn to read. Here, he reads the first three pages and shows how close his own reading is to the original text:

> Once there was an elephant. [Actual text: 'Once upon a time there was an elephant.']
>
> Once there was a little bad baby [Actual text: 'and one day the Elephant went for a walk and he met a Bad Baby. And the Elephant said to the Bad Baby, "Would you like a ride?" And the Bad Baby said, "Yes."']
>
> He said do you want a ride and the bad baby said yes. Went rumpeta, rumpeta, rumpeta all the way down the road. [Actual text: 'So the Elephant stretched out his trunk, and picked up the Bad Baby and put him on his back, and they went rumpeta, rumpeta, rumpeta, all down the road.']

The following day Anthony drew a picture of the elephant with people beside him (Figure 3.1) and retold the main events of the story as he drew:

> It's all the people chasing after the elephant. Tick tock. A long trunk. That's the end. He never said please for the food. The elephant sat down and slided off and all the people bumped into him.

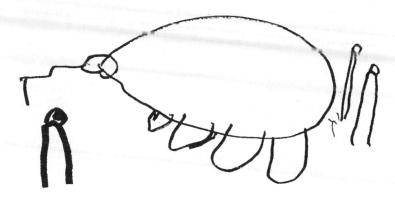

Figure 3.1

When Anthony had been in school for six months his enthusiasm for a current film helped to shed some light on his strong liking for the story of Little Red Riding Hood. Around this time he was watching the video of *Jaws* on television most Saturday mornings and he told me this story about himself and a shark as he drew a picture (Figure 3.2):

The shark bit me

This is the shark what bit me

Figure 3.2

That's me. Well, I've been doing a lot of fishing. I went fishing. A shark came up and it bit me right here where it's all swollen. [He pointed to a part of himself on the picture.] My dad put a bomb in its mouth and it blowed all to pieces. Going to put a bomb in his mouth and it blowed up. All the tooth came up one by one by one and picked them up and I threw the teeth away in the bin and all the blood came up. And I seen the belly come up.

Anthony is 'storying', inserting aspects of the story of *Jaws* into his own imaginary life experience. His drawings are a vehicle for him to express his ideas and feelings, holding the meaning steady while he takes the events of the story forward orally. His power as a narrator allows him to insert this intensely personal fictionalized account of himself going fishing, of being caught by the shark and then being rescued by his father, into the violent images he recalls from the film, taking his knowledge of this familiar media text he has seen at home forward into his school experience. In so doing he transforms terrifying events into a satisfying experience, with a happy ending for himself. The story seems to meet some inexpressible need in him, and the comparison with Little Red Riding Hood is striking. In both this shark story and in the Little Red Riding Hood story, a child is eaten by a savage beast, wolf or shark – metaphors for all that is dark and terrifying – and saved at the last minute by a courageous father. I believe this might have echoes in Anthony's own life. He doesn't actually live with his father, though he sees him from time to time, and he is possibly using the power of story to help him to consider his own future, hypothesizing about an idealized relationship with his father, who is always there to make things safe for him.

After two terms in school Anthony is controlling the pace of his own literacy learning, with support from home and school. Stories are centrally important to him in this enterprise, both those he reads and those he tells. While he is still a young inexperienced reader, he is at the same time a successful apprentice who has already learned a good deal about reading and writing from his early encounters with print. Stories give him pleasure, whether they're in books or on television, and his attempt to understand them in terms of his own life clearly involves him in levels of comprehension that go far beyond enjoyment.

Before Anthony came to school he already knew about stories (in books and on television), poems, newspapers, shopping lists, labels and titles. He had seen books treated with care and noted his

mother's and his sister's respect for literacy. At school now he has
no difficulty in using story to support his own fantasy games or to
script a hypothetical future for himself. He sees around him in his
classroom that same respect for literacy learning that he sees at
home and begins to ask questions about the way a book is set out.
His own path towards literacy has been defined, by home and by
school, and in one sense the way ahead is clear; yet I cannot help
but think that Anthony will take a hand in defining the route for
himself as he takes the next steps on the road to becoming a
reader.

• • •

Two years later Anthony still likes the story of Little Red Riding
Hood. 'I tell it to myself at night in my mind, in my sleep', he tells
me. 'I can't remember all the book. I can only remember in the
woods. The wolf comes first, then Little Red Riding Hood comes.'
He has a few books of his own now, including one featuring
Superman that he bought at Asda when he was shopping with his
mother. 'It's about evil and good', he says. 'Dark Storm is evil and
the other one's good. The Cheetah is good but he can't be the
leader. The lion's the leader, and I've got the little animal, like a
Cheetah, and you can move the legs. Fast-medium-slow speeds.'
Anthony loves watching films on video. One evening recently he
saw *Three Men and a Baby*. His mother said he liked it so much that
he watched it all through again the following morning on his own.
He needs no invitation to start telling me the story: 'It's about three
men. They can't look after the baby properly and the lady holds
him . . .'
   Anthony now has a younger brother; Anthony says he likes
reading because 'you can read to someone and if you've got a baby
brother you can read your book to them when you get older'. He
has identified an important purpose for reading, both now and in
the future. He explains: 'One day I got my reading book. I sat my
brother down beside me and I read it to him' (though his mother
says he seems frightened to say words he's reading in case he's
wrong). At school we sit and read together. He chooses John
Burningham's *Granpa* (1984) and points to the word 'sunshine'.
'That's one whole word', he tells me. He points to 'tomorrow' and
asks, 'Is that one whole word?' Then he turns the pages with confidence and his eyes follow the print as we read. He notices that
Burningham has used different fonts to represent the speech of

the girl and her grandfather. 'There's the girl speaking', he says, pointing to the text. I ask him how he knows. 'It's posh writing', he explains, and then shows me the print that represents Granpa's speech. Anthony's mother wishes he would read more. His main interest, she says, is in 'playing out and having sweets'. Sometimes she thinks she expects too much of him but at the same time she feels that he should do more reading, writing and maths. She has restricted his playing-out time so that he does some book work in the evening after his tea and he doesn't seem to object. 'One day I was going out to play and my mum told me off and said I have to learn. Now I do some work. Like sums and times tables. It's good 'cos then you can learn.'

His mother plays Scrabble with Paulette and he tries to join in, but finds it difficult, so she's going to buy him Junior Scrabble and play that with him. She doesn't often have time to read with him now, but he does pick up books on his own and watches Paulette doing her homework. His mother bought a novel from Woolworth's recently – her first for a long time. 'I could do with reading a good book', she explains. 'I want something to read at work instead of knitting all night when the patients are asleep.' The novel is about the Deep South. Anthony suddenly remembers he has a Transformer book. It's about Optimus Prime 'when he's very little'. And Anthony the storyteller tells another story:

> One day he went out in his truck and he went to this place and he didn't know the baddies lived there and they caught him. He thought the place he went to was the baddies', but it was the goodies', then he stayed with the proper goodies, then he grew up. Then he turned into a truck. Then he became a leader. And that's it.

4

GEETA

Geeta came into school cheerfully with her mother on her first morning. She wore a smart dress, as her mother wished, rather than the trousers she would really have preferred, and her long black hair was carefully plaited. Geeta confidently looked around for things to do and children she already knew. She had already spent a year in a nursery school and knew what to expect when she came into the classroom now: pictures on the wall, tables set out with Lego, paper, paints and crayons, and a corner with dressing-up clothes. She was used to choosing her own activities and at her nursery, after 'family time' in the morning, she often occupied herself with different tasks until dinner time without ever needing to go to see her teacher. Indeed, when I watched her playing in the nursery I saw a little girl who seemed very much at ease and totally confident, sitting at a table with six other children, five boys and one girl, building a tower with Lego. She held centre-stage, and was making the children laugh by knocking each block off one at a time with her nose.

Geeta's parents welcomed me warmly when I went to see them in their modern detached house, in a street of mainly older terraced housing towards the centre of town. We walked through the entrance hall into the front room, furnished with a modern three-piece suite, coffee table, music centre and plants. A large photograph of Geeta's grandfather stands on the fireplace and beside it is a photograph of the family's spiritual leader, Maharaj Charan Singh. A pair of large silvered giraffes stand elegantly at each end of the fireplace; Geeta's mother brought them back from India on her last visit. Angela, the eldest daughter, brings us tea and biscuits. Her father wears a suit and her mother is dressed in a shulwar kamiz; she's slim and delicately featured and complains of tiredness. Geeta comes to sit by me and we begin to talk about their hopes for their children. Geeta's parents believe that their children should be well educated, and are willing to spend time and money to give them the best opportunities they can afford. They decided to send Geeta to a nursery school because they felt she should 'sit down and learn and mix with other children' before she came to school. They feel that Geeta is clever and are ambitious for her, as they are for her two older sisters and older brother, now all at secondary schools in the city. Also, they are fully occupied in running their factory where they manufacture shirts and blouses, and they know they will not be able to give Geeta as many different experiences at home as she would receive in a nursery.

Even so, as the youngest child Geeta is treated 'like the baby in the family', says her mother, and she is given a great deal of attention. 'Everyone knows her name,' her mother adds, 'even the shopkeepers.' But she is particularly close to her mother who describes their mutually warm and supportive relationship like this:

> She is that close to me she even sleeps with me at night. I never love any other child like I do with her. I don't know why I felt like it, to be with her all the time . . . she still sleeps with me, one arm on top of my neck and the other under my neck. If I want to turn this side, she will turn before me; even if she is asleep, deep asleep, she will wake up.

Long before Geeta came to school she took herself seriously as a reader and had witnessed and joined in with a variety of reading and writing activities at home and at nursery school. At $4\frac{1}{2}$, about to enter school for the first time, she is already aware of the importance of reading and writing in the lives of people in her family. Her older sisters and brother unconsciously model book-reading and writing behaviour for her as she watches them doing their homework, and their attention to school-focused literacy shows her a pathway to her own future literacy learning. She observes them writing essays and notes and reading from textbooks, and she sometimes writes or draws alongside them. She sees her father writing letters, working on his accounts, making

notes, consulting the telephone directory; and she sees him reading holy books. She watches her mother and sisters reading for
pleasure, and at night Geeta and her mother read together in bed:
'If I go to bed at nine or nine-thirty I read a book, or a letter, or a
women's magazine, or an Indian newspaper, and Geeta will take
her own book', her mother explains. Geeta accompanies Ranu, her
11-year-old sister, to the library and chooses books there. 'She
doesn't know the ABC but she still brings a book', her mother says.
And it's Ranu who spends most time reading with her small sister.
'She's the only one in the family who's got the time to', says her
mother. 'You see, she doesn't have as much homework as the others.' Angela also reads with Geeta sometimes and tells me that
Geeta 'tries to read according to the pictures'. Geeta reads birthday
cards and wedding invitations when they arrive and she watches
advertisements on television. Her favourite is the one for 'Care
Bears'. Sometimes the family watches Indian films together on
video, and Geeta enjoys cartoons too.

Her mother was 12 or 13 when she came to England. She recalls
trying to learn English. 'I didn't even know the ABC', she explains.
She was taught English at school and now reads and writes in both
English and Punjabi. She remembers her parents reading from the
holy books, her mother and grandfather reading newspapers and
her father reading novels. In the Punjab on warm nights her family
slept on the flat roof of their house and listened to stories: 'Some
were so long they lasted many nights', she remembers. Geeta's
father recalls similar experiences, and although these storytelling
events are now part of their history, the family's inherited need for
a time to be close together and to share cultural and religious
experiences has endured and is fulfilled each day through their
religious observances. At half past eight each evening incense is lit,
and the family prays together. Sometimes one member reads from
a prayer book; at other times they tell me that 'if you know the
right words you don't have to open the book'. Afterwards the book
is respectfully covered with a cloth. The next morning, after washing or bathing, the cover is carefully removed. The family shares a
set of religious practices and beliefs set down in a book called *The
Master Answers* (1966). This contains the teachings of Maharaj
Charan Singh, who advocates a life of hard work, self-discipline
and meditation, in order to find inner peace with God. Sometimes
the family visits the Hindu temple if there is a particular festival
they want to observe; but since they feel that God is everywhere
around them they often choose to pray and meditate at home. I

was invited to look through their prayer book. It is a weighty volume, bound in leather and written in Punjabi. There are photographs in it of spiritual leaders and illustrations from Hindu stories. Geeta looked at the prayer book as I turned the pages and recognized an illustration of Rama and Sita. She will not be allowed to touch the book until she is older, although she did try to turn the pages as I held it, and was duly reprimanded. Reading this religious text has its own rules and patterns of family participation, and Geeta must abide by them.

At nursery Geeta's interest in books and stories has been fostered by her teacher. *John Brown, Rose and the Midnight Cat* (Wagner 1977) and *The Very Hungry Caterpillar* (Carle 1970) became her favourite picture-story books. She was encouraged to make writing patterns and to recognize her name card as her teacher held it up. Her teacher remarked that Geeta 'didn't have much interest in writing, but she liked drawing'. I watched her one day in the nursery as she drew a figure which she said was 'Daddy' (Figure 4.1). I asked Geeta if she could 'make it say Daddy in letters' and she wrote some marks above her drawing. Her writing is a mixture of signs, some little figures and a capital G. She already knows that writing has a symbolic function, that it stands for something else, and she is able to make her own script by inventing symbols for names. In this case, the symbols stand for 'Daddy'. This business of naming is crucially important to Geeta. Learning to name things and people, to say names, to write them, is to have control over them, to know them in a new way – and, central to all this, learning to make the letters of her own name, to see the letter G in front of her, and to be able to read it, gives Geeta a new control over language and an identity as a language user.

Three months before Geeta came to school, she and I read *Not Now Bernard* (McKee 1980) together. I chose this book because her nursery teacher had told me that Geeta knew and enjoyed the story. We sat side by side on the settee in her front room and as I read she attended closely, repeating my phrases and sometimes using them as cues to help her guess what came next, taking the reading on from me. Geeta is using her second language in this and subsequent extracts:

HM: 'Hello, Mum.'
Geeta: 'Hello, Mum. Not Now Bernard.'

She was obviously very familiar with the story:

HM: Who did he meet in the garden?

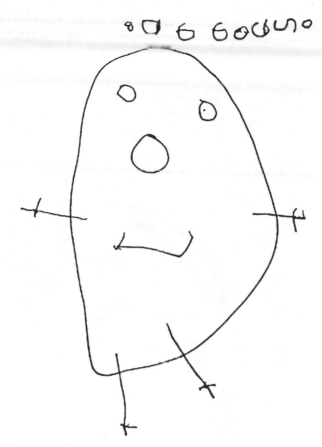

Figure 4.1   Daddy

Geeta: A monster.
HM: And what did he say to the monster?
Geeta: Hello, monster.
IIM: Hello, monster. And what did the monster do?
Geeta: Eat all up.
HM: Every bit of him.
Geeta: Every bit of him.

Geeta's eyes ranged over the pictures as we spoke just as Angela had noted, confirming for me how centrally important illustrations are in helping her to understand the story. She often commented skilfully and creatively on the pictures in the book, making

a sequence of events from what she saw and occasionally repeating my words and phrases – 'every bit of him'; as an emergent bilingual learner, the repetition of everyday phrases like this is an
important strategy that helps her to learn the syntax of English. It

Figure 4.2   Geeta's drawing of a monster – and her writing

also helps her to understand the meaning of the text. Later she commented on an illustration of Bernard's mother:

Geeta: She's got . . . and she's watering the plants and she's wetting all the plants.

Geeta's close scrutiny of pictures helps her to make sense of a story in her own terms and gives her an opportunity of talking about a book, thus extending her use of English. She has learned this strategy from her story-telling sessions with Angela and her teachers at nursery school and from her experience of media literacy; watching television films and cartoons has shown her how to match visual clues with words in order to make meaning. She will bring this knowledge and skill with her to her book-reading at school.

Later that same afternoon Geeta decided to draw the monster from the story (Figure 4.2). When she had completed the huge shape, she proceeded to draw some Gs up the left-hand edge of the monster. She said these were 'my name'. She then drew some number 3s in the top left-hand corner, and some upside-down As in the bottom corner opposite. Down the left-hand side she drew a long curly line, saying it was T, E and B. These letters are distributed randomly around her drawing, seeming to fill in the space. There is no linearity; she writes where she chooses to, using the letter and number shapes she knows. She seems to be at the stage of *drawing letters and numbers*; and she draws the letter G to stand for one word, her name, thus keeping herself quite literally at the centre of her own learning experience.

At school Geeta uses her social and story-making skills to plan and create a fictional world for herself and her friends in the playhouse. She opens the dressing-up box with great gusto and dons a white hat, oblivious to all around her. She gives her friend Sherine a handbag. First they decide on their roles and responsibilities.

Sherine: Come on, Mum.
Geeta: I'm not Mum. We're two sisters.
Sherine: You hold the dog. I'll have the baby [she gets a doll out of the box for herself and a toy dog for Geeta].
Geeta: We both have babies [she reaches in the box for another doll]. This is my baby and I'll have the dog too. I'm going to the park.

At this point they walk in celebratory fashion around the classroom, holding their babies and pulling the dog along behind them.

They are joined by two more children and then it is time, of course, for tea. Sherine and Geeta support each other in creating this make-believe world through their use of language to organize the story they invent for themselves. Geeta's mastery of narrative form enables her to do this well and she takes on the roles of both mother and sister as she builds a context for the events to take place in.

When Geeta has been at school for about three months she begins to ask questions about the way books are written. One day we had this conversation about *The Snowman* (Briggs 1978), a book without a written text, where the story is told entirely through the illustrations:

Geeta:	What's that say? [pointing to the title]
HM:	'The Snowman'
Geeta:	The Snowman. That's all said Snowman? [she points to the title]
HM:	[I nod] And that says Raymond Briggs [I point to his name].
Geeta:	He wrote that?
HM:	He wrote . . . he made the pictures and it was his idea for the story.
Geeta:	He wrote The Snowman? All of this?
HM:	Mmm. He drew all the pictures for the book and he had the idea for the story.
Geeta:	I haven't seen him.
HM:	No. I've seen a picture of him but I've never seen him in real life.
Geeta:	How did he make this, then?
HM:	I think he had a good idea for a story, and he's a very good artist, and he started to draw all the pictures for the book.

Geeta is beginning to grapple with the idea that stories are invented, written by people. She offers her own retelling of the book and tells me that 'The Snowman haven't got words' and that she will 'just have to get some words' in order to read the story. Geeta's conscious use of the word 'words' shows me that she is beginning to learn about metalanguage, the language to talk about language. She knows that language is made up of separate words, and when she announces that she will 'just have to get some words', she becomes the re-creator and the authorial voice for the book, matching her own words with those of the illustrations in the book. Here is the beginning of her story:

There's a boy, he's gone to sleep and it's snowing and he just dress up and he looking out the window. It's snowing and he pulls his boots on and go outside and he left his hat off because he making big ball a snowman. He getting nose nose and eyes and mouth. He get the mouth, put it with the finger in the mouth and he just nearly finished . . .

There is a memory of a previous retelling in Geeta's head and she brings *The Snowman* to life all over again by shaping the illustrations into a story with her own language. I am her audience, and listen silently. She continues to tell the story in this fashion, looking perceptively at each illustration, until she reaches the end:

. . . so he's gone to seaside to fly away and he and snowman said oh and he came back home and he and he get out and he wake up and he couldn't sleep and he gone downstairs gone upstairs and downstairs. The snowman was melt.

Not long after this *The Jolly Postman* (Ahlberg and Ahlberg 1986) became one of Geeta's favourite books, and her shared reading of this story uncovers more about her developing reading knowledge. We sit together looking at the page where the postman brings the letter from Goldilocks to the three bears:

Geeta: Three bears. One daddy one, one mummy one. We got three bears of that haven't we?

Geeta is looking closely at the illustration and recognizes the three bears as the same bears she knows from the traditional fairy story. She shows that she understands about the intertextual link between stories as she recalls that we have another book with the story of Goldilocks in – 'We got three bears of that haven't we?' In other words, she is discovering that the three bears can appear in more than one version of a story, and still remain the same bears. I read what it says on the envelope:

HM: And it says 'Mr and Mrs Bear, Three Bears Cottage, The Woods.'
Geeta: The Woods.

Geeta repeats 'The Woods' after me and waits for me to continue:

HM: . . . and if you open it up . . .
Geeta: Yeah . . .
HM: It says –

Now Geeta takes over the reading and has a go at remembering what the letter says, rehearsing the letter's formal introduction with her reading of 'dear three bears':

Geeta: Bear Cottages. Get for letter for dear three bears.

I help her out and continue reading. As I read she ghosts the words quietly and joins in with 'your house' and 'says':

HM: 'Dear Mr and Mrs Bear and baby bear. I am very sorry indeed that I came to *your house*'
Geeta: *your house*
HM: 'and ate baby bear's porridge. Mummy says I am a bad girl. I hardly eat any porridge when she cooks it she *says*'
Geeta: *says*
HM: 'Daddy says he will mend the little chair. Love from Goldilocks. PS Baby bear –'

Geeta interjects at this point. She seems to need me to stop while she makes sense of what has happened so far. She returns to the illustrations again:

Geeta: That's the daddy one that's the mummy one the baby one [she points to three bowls of jelly on Goldilocks's letter] Where she's coming sunshine and sky up there [she points to the picture of the sun and sky on Goldilocks's letter]

Then Geeta goes on to do something that shows me she is beginning to recognize individual words when she says: 'and there's a "like" . . . a "like" somewhere. I saw it here.' I ask her to clarify what she means:

HM: Like. You mean the word 'like'?
Geeta: Like
HM: Like?
Geeta: I and like.

I scan the text for 'like' and find 'likes'. I point to it:

HM: There's 'likes'.
Geeta: Yeah, oh yeah.

And so we have a conversation about the book at two levels. There's the story itself that we remake together, with its networks into other stories Geeta knows, and there's the conversation about the word 'like', which we discuss using specialized language ourselves.

Geeta does not read at home with her parents. They are extremely busy running their factory and feel, in any case, that if she needs help then her older brother and sisters are there to assist her. Here, Ranu and Geeta read a version of the Little Red Riding Hood story together at home into a tape-recorder. Geeta, in fact, does most of the storytelling and Ranu supports her by whispering a word or phrase if she hesitates, thus ensuring that Geeta's reading sounds fluent, effortless and uncorrected for this taped performance. Because she is supported in this way, Geeta is exuberant and inventive. Here is part of her retelling:

Geeta: Goodbye, says Red Riding Hood's mummy. If you saw your daddy, if that Big Bad Wolf gets you tell your daddy to come back for tea. Little Red Riding Hood said to her grandmother which flowers she likes.

I sense that Ranu is slightly uncomfortable with Geeta's interpretation of the story and would prefer her to try and read the actual words, so she brings Geeta back to the text. Geeta repeats the words after her but then continues with her own retelling. Ranu's reading of 'Little Red Riding Hood sees some trees' is immediately repeated by Geeta, and Ranu acts as a good role model for her younger sister's development of English syntax:

Ranu: 'Little Red Riding Hood sees some trees.'
Geeta: Little Red Riding Hood sees some trees and some flowers. She said grandmother likes flowers.

Ranu whispers the text to her again very quietly, but the words of the text are not what Geeta needs at this moment: 'I can make up this to read', she insists. The version of the story she wants is in her head, along with some of the literary language she has remembered from previous readings:

Geeta: I can make up this to read. She see up to the . . . she see the big bad wolf and he near a tree. He said play with me. Play with me. I can't. I can't. I have to see the grandmother. Erm . . . I got cakes and flowers for grandmother.

The language of books is often complex and Geeta struggles with the syntax of written English. But Ranu seems to accept Geeta's version and now sensitively corrects her only when individual words change the meaning for her:

Geeta: I see . . . the wolf gets . . .
Ranu: goes . . .
Geeta: goes to Grandmother's . . .
Ranu: home . . .
Geeta: home. Grandmother. Knock. Knock. Grandmother. Knock. Knock. Little Red Riding Hood. Come in she says. She see the big bad wolf. She gets to the . . .
Ranu: cupboard . . .
Geeta: cupboard. Help. Help. What she says?

The two girls continue in this fashion until they reach the end of the story. Geeta is so enthusiastic, so much in control of the way she wants to put her version of the story across, that Ranu has to be quick and clever to anticipate her needs, though I sense she is perhaps frustrated by Geeta's lack of attention to the text itself.

At school Geeta's teacher also meets Geeta's reading needs as she shares a book with her, attending to all her queries and setting up a comfortable reading context where Geeta feels at ease to ask about anything that might be puzzling her. Her teacher introduces a book by telling Geeta what the title is, and it is significant that Geeta comes in immediately with a query about the author. Her teacher has made Geeta feel comfortable enough to ask about things that puzzle her by giving her equal rights to speak and ask questions and by being a good listener. She has to decide how best to explain the concept of authorship to the 4-year-old:

Teacher: 'The Noisiest Class in School'. By Pauline Hill.
Geeta: Pauline Hill.
Teacher: That's Pauline Hill wrote the words in the book, wrote the story.
Geeta: All the pictures?
Teacher: No. The pictures, the illustrations, were by Joan Beales.
Geeta: Joan Beales.
Teacher: That's another lady.
Geeta: That's another lady.
Teacher: It is, yes.
Geeta: Who drew the pictures?
Teacher: Joan Beales.
Geeta: Joan Beales.

Geeta is tenacious in her quest for information, repeating phrases and names after her teacher, practising the grammatical structure of these phrases, and drawing on her teacher's knowledge. There would have been no room for Geeta's preoccupation with these matters if her teacher had set the reading situation up differently, perhaps by expecting her to listen silently as she read the story to her. When she is satisfied that Geeta has understood a little more about what an author and an illustrator do she hands the next reading task to Geeta, giving her responsibility for turning the page. 'That's right. Go on then. You turn the next page over', she says invitingly. She knows that Geeta is knowledgeable about handling a book, and is able to turn the page for herself. This simple act also gives Geeta the responsibility for turning over in her own time, looking first at whatever interests her on each new page. Geeta's role in this story-reading session is active; she knows it's her job to get meaning from the book with the support of her teacher by making comments and asking questions. Her teacher helps her by giving her an explanation for things she doesn't understand. These learning conditions also enable Geeta to ask about new vocabulary she has not met before. She listens carefully and wants an explanation for everything she doesn't understand, working in collaboration with her teacher to make meaning from the text. Here, working again as an emergent bilingual, she demonstrates her interest in words themselves as she discovers and worries away at the word 'tatty' in order to find out what it means. Her questioning demonstrates that it would be naive for writers, teachers and publishers to assume that words like 'tatty' are part of the vocabulary of emergent bilinguals:

Teacher: 'Dirty Bert, with his tatty shirt –'
Geeta: What does tatty mean?
Teacher: Tatty? Untidy. Not very nice.
Geeta: Not very nice?
Teacher: A bit ripped, might be, tatty. Or a bit creased.
Geeta: Like this? [she looks at her own blouse]
Teacher: A bit creased like that, yes. But that isn't really tatty. That's creased, because you've been wearing it all day.

Satisfied that she understands a little of what 'tatty' means, Geeta's teacher begins to read the next page, where she finds that Geeta responds to the information in the story by matching it against her own experience in order to make sense of it. Just as Geeta used the example of her own blouse to enhance her understanding of the word 'tatty', she has the skill to find a way of matching other incidents in the book to her own experience:

Teacher: 'Our school has got a bus. It picks us all up each morning and takes us to school.'
Geeta: My dad goes to the factory and my mum and she come back to fetch me and goes back to the factory to eat her dinner.

Geeta's teacher could have led her back to the book at this point, but she decides to continue the conversation because she knows that it matters to her. Geeta does not arrive at school on a bus and the story gives her a way of framing her own day by reflecting on the way she is brought to school and collected at night and, by extension, telling the story of her mother's day and of a broken coffee machine:

Teacher: She has her dinner at the factory?
Geeta: No, she brings her dinner at the factory 'cos we haven't got no dinners at the factory. We just got the coffee. We still haven't got any coffee, right. We got the machine of it so we got a new one. We got an old one, it's broke. It doesn't work for six months.

This shared book-reading shows clearly that the meaning does not lie in the printed words alone. Indeed, meaning has to be brought to life by Geeta as she searches for experiences in her own life that shed light on her understanding of the story. Geeta matches her own experiences against those of the children in the story and in doing so she makes sense of her own world and the world of the book. The story about the broken coffee machine, from her own world, helps her to make sense of her mother's experience at work. Geeta's teacher allows her time to tussle with the meaning of each page in this fashion. Her response depends on what Geeta has noticed in the text or the illustrations, what she has understood or was confused by, and how she interprets the story in terms of her own life. This way of setting up and maintaining a story-reading session allows Geeta to trust her teacher by asking her questions, becoming a conversational partner. As Geeta examines her own life she develops a deeper understanding of the learning process itself, discovering that she is free to move away from the story if she wishes and that the meaning she brings to the story is valid. Further on in the story, on a page that shows the children painting pictures, Geeta pays attention to two elements of a picture-story book that we know are important to her: the illustrations and individual words and letters. She finds a way of attending to both, assisted by her teacher, and of volunteering her own information:

Teacher: 'Do we like painting? Our class does.'
Geeta· We do paintings. We do paints. He's got a nice one, she's got a nice one [she points to the paintings].
Teacher: They've all written their names on the paintings.
Geeta: Looks like my name up there [she points to the word 'Gene'].
Teacher: Yes.Your name begins with that letter.
Geeta: Yes. You've got two of those in your name [she points to the two Es in 'Gene'].
Teacher: Yes. A G and two Es. Gene's got a G and two Es in his name.

Geeta, encouraged by her teacher, demonstrates that she is beginning to understand how sounds and symbols function together. She could not, of course, read this book without the help of her teacher, who makes the author's words available to her by reading them aloud, and then makes it possible for Geeta to respond to the reading in this active way. Geeta interrogates every page in the book, and in so doing learns to establish connections between her own first-hand experience and the experience she comes across in the story, something she must continue to do in her head when she is a silent, independent reader. I am continually impressed by Geeta's ability to collaborate with someone else in order to make sense of what she is reading. She seems to know intuitively how and when she needs to do this, and the kinds of questions she needs to ask in order to move her understanding forward.

As I observe Geeta I see a child in control of her own language learning, who is intensely curious about things she doesn't understand and knows how to use adults to help her gain information. These observations suggest that Geeta is well on her way to becoming a reader, even though she has yet to achieve mastery of the alphabetic nature of written language. Her conscious awareness of herself as a language user, and of language itself as an object for discussion and use, are evidence of the high expectations she has of herself. She talks about language and about herself as a language user constantly – 'When I'm big I'll write a sentence', and 'when I'm big I'll write a hard story', I overhear her telling her teacher from time to time, confident of her own future success as a scholar, and once again using a specialized word – 'sentence' – to talk about language itself.

Geeta is moving to a point in her language development where she is paying attention to meaning and at the same time making connections about language and about the form that books take. Her approach to literacy was shaped before she came to school by the social practices of her home and nursery school, and there is little doubt that she wants to be as successful as her brothers and sisters. The particular social and literacy patterns of her home, her familiarity with books, her interest in story and pictures, her encounters with religious literacy, all underlie her early reading experiences and help me to understand the high expectations she has of herself as a future reader and writer.

• • •

Two years later Geeta still loves listening to stories at school; her favourite story at the moment is *Meg and Mog* (Nicoll and Pienkowski 1972). She mixes well and likes to use her knowledge of language and reading to 'play teacher' with a group of children, telling them a story and at other times leaning over their shoulders when they are reading to prompt them if they are stuck on a word. Her teacher says she knows a great deal about books and is very interested in the alphabetic nature of written language. Even so, she is not yet able to trust herself to read independently, though her teacher feels the knowledge she needs is there in her head. She is fascinated by the keyboard on the word-processor and loves to study it. 'How do you get a capital letter?' she asked her teacher when she was first introduced to the machine.

Her mother says Geeta can read if she concentrates but she 'makes silly mistakes'. She says she believes children are motivated to learn either through fear or through jealousy, and that Geeta has not yet been motivated sufficiently in either of these areas to want to learn sufficiently well. She spends a great deal of time at home colouring, mostly houses and people, and says she wants to be a wrestler when she grows up. Her older brother writes sums out for her and Ranu still reads with her, though she doesn't have so much time now that she has more homework. Geeta's older brother and sisters all had private tuition from an Indian teacher who taught them 'English and grammar', and Geeta is beginning lessons with this teacher too. This will mean she has no time to go to the library.

Geeta still loves cartoons, which she watches on the children's channel of cable television. Mickey Mouse is her favourite. She also likes watching *The Cosby Show*, *Home and Away* and *Neighbours*. If she hears a song once on television, she's 'got it', her mother says, but she really feels that Geeta watches too much television. The family views Indian films together on video and they are particularly interested in the cycle of Hindu films of the Gita. Geeta is not yet interested in religious books but her mother is not anxious about this and feels she is still 'too young to look at the books, though she knows about Rama and Sita'.

5

REID

Four weeks after he started school Reid told me, 'I'm good at writing if someone showed me how to write. I can do number 4s.' He drew a picture and watched me making notes as I sat by him. What he said about himself shows his ability to be reflective, his confidence in himself as a learner and his expectation that he can and will learn from people who know more than he does. This attitude is firmly embedded in the kinds of learning that happen in his home, where Reid is involved in learning things from his parents and his older brother and sister.

Reid's parents believe that school provides their children with the values and attitudes they will need in order to work hard and achieve success. They hold strong beliefs about the way learning should be fostered in their home and make every effort to provide a stimulating environment for their children to grow up in. Their cultural assumptions match those of schools and their views are familiar and similar to those held by many professional educationalists. 'We look for the learning potential in everything', Reid's mother explains. 'We believe in spending time constructively and creatively as a way of preparing the children for life.' They feel that Reid had already had 'quite a varied sort of experience of life' and have taken him to the seaside, zoos and bird sanctuaries, to museums, antique fairs and insect fairs. The family goes ice skating and swimming together and regularly visits friends and relations.

Reid's mother even exploits the learning opportunities which a shopping trip affords: 'I see it as a special time for Reid to be with me on my own, just mother and son together. I did the same with Amber when she was smaller. I get Reid to feel as if he's part of the expedition, and quite an important part as well.' She might ask him to choose a packet of biscuits, but it has to be 'a sort we all like, so he's got to think about it'. In this way she encourages his sense of social responsibility towards the rest of the family.

Reid lives in a large ivy-covered Edwardian cottage in Hall Green on the north-east boundary of the city. It isn't in the school's catchment area, but when the family moved house a few years ago they requested that the children should stay at their present school. They have worked hard to make the cottage comfortable and attractive, collecting antiques and designing colour schemes and furnishings with care, and planning the cottage garden. In the household everyone's interests are fostered and supported, talked about and shared. Reid's father, a precision engineer by trade, loves anything to do with the natural world, and insects in particular. 'It's something I never grew out of', he says. 'I'm like a child.' He has an impressive collection of insects in a polished Victorian cabinet, all carefully labelled and documented. The family watches nature programmes together on television, and on holiday they pick and identify flowers, go 'rock-pooling', collect skulls, watch birds, and help each other to use information books and field guides to identify what they see and collect. 'It's bred into them to enjoy the nature side of it', Reid's father explains. His other passion is the music of Frank Zappa. He keeps a scrapbook about Zappa and owns all his albums. He once wrote to the singer, telling him that Reid's middle name is Zappa and enclosing a copy of his birth certificate with photos and information about the family. He is still disappointed that Frank Zappa did not reply.

I visit Reid's home at about eight o'clock in the evening, so that Reid's mother has had time to put the children to bed. We sit in the lounge and talk. It's a cosy room, furnished with easy chairs, a music centre and a television. There's an aquarium in the alcove and records and tapes are stored on shelves. Reid's mother is a trained nursery nurse and works in a school for handicapped children. Last year she studied A-level English in her own time and for her own interest, and she is considering taking a teacher-training course. She also paints, etches and once wrote a children's story. She also wrote a book of poems and dedicated them to Liam, her eldest son. She loves poetry and 'sometimes as we're going along in the car, if something triggers it off, I suddenly start bursting into

Thomas Love Peacock or Wilfred Owen or something! I've always loved to repeat poems. I can repeat nearly every poem I've ever had to learn.' I note that Reid will have been exposed to different kinds of literature before he comes to school and will probably know about the value placed on memorizing particular texts.

Literacy for Reid is embedded in his daily life. He sees an unusually wide variety of reading and writing around him in his home, and is invited to share a good deal of this. He observes his parents and older brother and sister reading and writing for various purposes and in different ways. Books are inseparable from the life of the family and are accorded high status within the household. Pinned to a board in the kitchen are bills that need paying, pools coupons, lists of jobs to do, invitations to parties or weddings, E additives and diet sheets and tickets for dances or concerts. There's a kitchen calendar where Reid's mother jots down reminders about birthdays, dentist's appointments and so on. The kitchen drawers are filled with writing paper and envelopes, cards to send, address and telephone books, club books and an Argos catalogue, together with all the paperwork for the mail order club. Reid's mother keeps an exercise book in which she's written an extended shopping list of 'every single thing we ever use' and she uses this as a checklist. In addition, she writes at least two letters a week and one full page in her diary every day. Reid has always been encouraged to write for himself; he writes his own name on birthday cards and sends off for things on cereal packets. In return, he receives birthday cards and free gifts like tennis balls and tapes, all personally addressed to him. There is a list of stolen car numbers in the family car. These are taken from the *Coventry Evening Telegraph*, and the children are encouraged to read number plates as they drive along, hoping to spot a stolen car. Maps and caravan handbooks and holiday brochures are also kept in the car and caravan.

All three children have their own individual bedrooms, and each room upstairs has its own bookshelves. In their cottage there has been space to make one of their upstairs rooms into a library, with a large comfortable settee, bookshelves, books, posters, games, toys in boxes, notice boards, certificates and engraved trophies. The family goes to book sales at the local library and they come away with so many cheap books that 'we clean the library out usually'. The children keep some books in their own bedrooms but they are encouraged to keep their books in the upstairs library so that they remain in good condition. Reid's father describes himself as a bookworm: 'I think reading's terrific', he says. 'Franz

Kafka. Trying to read all through that. Heavy going, but good. Science Fiction. Tolkien. Got them all. Nature, butterfly books. Reference books. Got them all.'When he was a boy he had his own library.'I've still got some of the books', he says.'I used to put numbers in them and sit at a little desk and lend them out to people with a little ticket.' Reid's mother loves Shakespeare and poetry and enjoyed some of the novels she read for English A-level. Mostly, though, she reads information and reference books, usually to do with different child handicaps in connection with her work as a nursery nurse. She is also interested in books about the Second World War.

It seems that Reid is growing up in an environment where reading and writing are central to the way the family lives.'Right from when he was small there's always been so many books about that he's always felt at home with books', says his mother. In the upstairs library he has watched Amber, aged 7, browsing through books, and now spends time doing this himself. Sometimes all three children go to this special room and sit on the settee with a pile of books each. As well as choosing picture-story books, Reid likes to read his brother's dinosaur books or his father's butterfly or insect books. In the public library Reid chooses his own books.'We make it an enjoyable experience for them and they sit on the little chairs and look through the books', his mother says. Reid begins to understand a little of the story of his own life and his family's history, as he looks through the family photograph album with his parents.'You tell stories of their life really', his parents explain, and his mother shows him photographs of relations and of herself as a little girl. In this way Reid makes sense of the passage of time, learning that he has a past and that his mother has too.

Reid's parents both feel that it is important for the children to have a bedtime story. Their own happy memories of being read to as children make this an activity they want their own children to share.'My mum used to take me in her bed at night and read or tell me a story about when she was a little girl', Reid's mother explains. His father also has a vivid memory of shared stories.'Dad was mad on telling me stories. I can remember always getting told a story', he says, and now he reads or tells a bedtime story to Reid and Amber every night. While Reid waits for his father to finish reading to Amber, he sits in bed and looks at a book by himself, and he may carry on looking at a book when his father has finished reading to him. Sometimes Reid chooses the book to be read, and at other times his father chooses it. Occasionally Reid's father makes up a story for Reid and Amber: 'I usually have them two in it', he explains. Like many young children, Reid enjoys the same book over and over again: 'When he was 2 he wanted *Good Morning Baby Bear* [Hill 1984], oh God, every single night!', his mother remembers with humour and not a little exasperation.

When Reid shares a book with his parents he is encouraged to enter into the kind of interactive dialogue that his parents feel will help him to understand the story. Before he came to school he was already sharing picture books regularly with his mother. Here, three months before Reid is due to come to school, they read *That Fat Cat* (Evans 1985) together. This book belongs to the family and Reid has heard it before. They are in the front room, because this is where the tape recorder is, though normally Reid reads upstairs with his mother. She begins by encouraging him to recall the title:

Mother: Do you know what this book's called?
Reid: Yes, the cat got stuck in . . .

She acknowledges his attempt and begins to read to him. She has a clear view of how she wants to share a book so that Reid will learn and enjoy the story at the same time. She controls the story-reading session carefully by eliciting certain responses from Reid at key points in the story and often looks ahead to pinpoint particular strategies she can use to help him understand:

Mother: 'That Fat Cat' it's called. So you were nearly right, weren't you? 'Once upon a time there was a big fat cat, called Kafka. He was very lazy. What he liked to do best was to sit in front of the fire and sleep. And when he wasn't sleeping he liked to eat. He ate two big cans of cat food every day, and drank three saucers of milk.'

Reid interjects as she finishes the page, asking: 'Mum, can I have a swim in my pool when it's warm?' He has not long come back from swimming with his father and this surely prompts his remark, which is quite unconnected with the story. Perhaps he is not in the mood for reading and is trying to divert his mother's attention away from the task, somehow needing to keep a foothold in the real world by firmly resisting the world of the book. His mother allows this diversion, and has to work hard to try and understand what he's getting at as he goes on to say:

Reid: Toys used to be in there.
Mother: Used to be in where?
Reid: The swimming bath.

Mother: What? In town?
Reid: What?
Mother: In town. The swimming baths in town where you've just been?
Reid: Yes. Well, toys used to be in the swimming baths.
Mother: I don't remember. What sort of toys?
Reid: Well, boats. Small boats.
Mother: Was there?
Reid: Yeah.
Mother: I don't remember.
Reid: When I went there, when I went there I saw some toys there.
Mother: Did you? Right then. Shall we carry on with the story now?

Reid's mother isn't sure what he is trying to tell her and she asks him a series of questions to help make his meaning clear. This conversation shows how she respects and values his talk, even though it does not seem to have any relevance to the task in hand. When the time seems right, she takes Reid back to the book. As she reads she pauses every so often to ask him questions about the text in order to find out if he's understood it:

Mother: 'So the next day, Daddy gave Kafka just half a tin of cat food and one saucer of milk.' Do you think he'd be very happy about this?
Reid: No.
Mother: Why?
Reid: 'Cos he wants to eat he wants to have loads.

She takes the opportunity of helping Reid to match his knowledge of the story with the memory of his own favourite foods, bringing the story world and his own world closer together and helping him understand the predicament of the cat in the story:

Mother: He wants to have loads and loads. A bit like you then isn't he, really?
Reid: No!
Mother: Oh well you have loads and loads of dinner, don't you?
Reid: I don't have loads and loads of ice cream.
Mother: Don't you? You're always saying to me ... what do you say?
Reid: I want a sweetie!
Mother: So you're a bit like Kafka. You might get fat like him if you eat like you do.

Reid's mother helps him to anticipate what will happen next in the story, and her pause encourages him to complete the sentence:

Mother: '. . . but when he tries to get out of the flap . . .'
Reid: . . . He couldn't get out.

Later on in the story, the name of one of the child characters takes Reid's mother into a conversation with Reid about his auntie. This time she initiates the discussion and she takes Reid out of the text while they talk about their family together:

Mother: 'So Granny called the children.' Do you remember their names?
Reid: Tim and . . . erm . . . Jane.
Mother: Yes. That's like my sister, isn't it. Jane?
Reid: Yes.
Mother: Where does Jane live?
Reid: Jane lives a long way away.
Mother: A long way away . . . and who lives with Jane?
Reid: Gary.
Mother: . . . and . . . you've forgotten somebody. Jane, Gary and little
           . . .
Reid: Lois.
Mother: Lois, that's right.

Mention of the baby causes Reid to comment: 'I wish we had a baby.' His mother acknowledges his comment and reminds Reid that Lois did come to stay with them. Reid misunderstands her reply; if there was a baby in the house it must have been when he or Amber were babies themselves:

Mother: Do you? Well, we did have her for one night, didn't we?
Reid: Yes. That was me and Amber being the baby.

His mother realizes that he has misunderstood and attempts to help him:

Mother: No. We had Lois sleeping here, didn't we? Remember?
Reid: Yes.
Mother: She was a good baby, wasn't she?
Reid: We never waked her up.
Mother: Oh no. 'Cos you were so good as well.
Reid: I just was going upstairs to bed and I never woke her up.

They return to the story and Reid's mother signals that they have nearly reached the end:

Mother: Shall we just finish the end of the story, see if they all got
what they wanted?

She sees an occasion for encouraging Reid to pay attention to
the words on the page. This is the only time in the story, apart from
reading the title, where she has drawn his attention to the actual
text:

Mother: I want you to help me remember what they all wanted
now. 'The mouse had . . .'
Reid: cheese.
Mother: 'and the dog had a . . .'
Reid: . . . bone.
Mother: 'Jane had . . .'
Reid: cake.

And so the story ends happily. Throughout, Reid's mother has controlled the story-reading session by eliciting certain responses
from Reid at various points. She has a clear sense of what she
wants him to do as they read together and uses particular strategies to achieve this. Reid, at the same time, is learning that a story-
reading session involves knowing that a book has a title, listening
to an adult reading, guessing some of the words when invited to do
so, remembering how a story goes if it is one he has heard before
and using events from his own life to match against the events of
the story and discussing these. He knows it is perfectly valid for
him to deviate from the text if this seems appropriate and he
expects to be listened to by the person reading the story. When
Reid starts school he will probably have similar expectations about
the way grown-ups will share books with him in the classroom.

Here, eight weeks after starting school, Reid and I read *Where the
Wild Things Are* (Sendak 1970) together. He already knows the
story well and wants to share and celebrate his previous knowledge of it with me. He likes the story and he knows that I like it. I
invite him to tell me the title, just as his mother did when she
introduced *That Fat Cat* and we set up a context for the reading
time together. He is used to being included in decision-making
processes at home and is prepared to ask me for what he wants.
'Can you read it to me?' he asks, and I nod agreement, though I
want to give Reid the opportunity of taking over parts of the reading if he wishes, so I say: 'You join in where you want to.' It is very
important to involve Reid in these negotiations about how a book
should be read, because in this way he is being kept at the centre of
his own learning and thinking processes, made fully conscious of

his own role as a reader. He will be able to decide what he feels able to do alone and what he has to do in order to get the support he needs from a teacher. I begin to read and Reid almost immediately feels comfortable enough to join in and take over the telling of the story:

HM:	'The night Max wore his wolf suit and made mischief of one kind –'
Reid:	And his room changes into a forest.

He's telling himself the story all over again. He remembers what Max says, then tells me what will happen to Max's bedroom:

Reid:	I'm gonna eat you . . .
HM:	'. . . and another. His mother called him Wild Thing and Max said I'll eat you up, and so he was sent to bed without eating anything. That very night in Max's room a forest grew . . .'
Reid:	I bet it's going to be part of the grass [he points to Max's bedroom carpet].
HM:	The carpet?
Reid:	I bet it's going to be the part of the grass.
HM:	*It is!*
Reid:	*Yes, it is!*

Long before Reid came to school he had made the discovery that the story world in the book stays the same across readings and across time, and this knowledge enables him to hold Max's fictional world steady while sharing the book with me. Reid has always been invited by his parents to respond to stories in ways which give him full participatory rights in the interpretation of both text and illustrations, and he continues to respond in this way when he shares a book with an adult at school. His previous readings of this story have given him a memory for the narrative, and although he knows that the carpet will become the grass (and probably knows that I know) he nevertheless wants to present the information to me as though it is a surprise for both of us. I think he does this as a way of celebrating his knowledge and his memory of the story. I carry on reading and Reid joins in again when he feels he wants to, confident and relaxed:

HM:	'. . . a forest grew and grew . . .'
Reid:	and grew . . . till it . . .
HM:	'till his ceiling hung with vines and the walls became the world all around . . .'

Reid: He founded a pirate a pirate boat for him.
HM: 'That night . . .'
Reid: And it says Max.
HM: Yes. 'And he sailed off through night and day . . .'

Reid's substitution of 'pirate' for 'private' shows me that he is attending closely to the meaning of the text. The word 'private' is used in the text to describe Max's boat but might not yet be part of Reid's personal vocabulary. Perhaps this is why he mishears 'private' as 'pirate'. After all, he does know about pirate boats, and a pirate boat is fully in keeping with Max's adventure. Reid also reads the name painted on the private boat in the illustration – 'and it says Max' – showing that he is beginning to pay attention to individual words in the text.

No adult, at home or at school, has ever put Reid in the position of feeling that he will not succeed as a reader. He has always been encouraged to follow his inclination to make sense of what he reads. The messages he receives are that reading is something for him; something he is entitled to as of right, and something that is achievable. Three weeks after coming to school he tells me about his books: 'I've got thousands of books at home,' he says, 'in my bedroom and in the library room.' The attention paid to written language in his home has helped him to begin to understand how language functions, and to identify himself as a language user. He knows the meaning of 'word' when he tells me: 'I can't read really. Amber shows me how to read but I can't read this. I can't really read. Amber shows me how I can read. How I can really read so I can do the words.' His growing interest in the meaning of language can be seen when he asks his teacher about a particular word when he and Anthony, also 4½, read *Mr Gumpy's Outing* (Burningham 1970) with her, and she understandably mishears his question concerning the word 'bleeding':

Anthony: Can I go, said the sheep.
Teacher: 'Yes, but don't keep bleating.'
Reid: What's bleating mean?
Teacher: That's the sound the sheep make. When it goes baa-baa, we call that bleating.
Reid: I thought you said bleeding.
Teacher: No. Bleating.

Reid demonstrates his growing interest in individual words and their meaning and also in the overall meaning of the story, by isolating this word from the text and asking for an explanation; pre-

sumably he can't understand why the sheep should be 'bleeding' –
the sheep in the picture appears to be perfectly well. He understands the teacher's explanation but his misunderstanding serves
as a reminder that careful articulation of unusual or infrequently
used words that might be difficult to predict, is important for *all*
readers, and perhaps particularly so for emergent bilingual learners. As the story progresses Reid leaves his classroom behind as he
enters the world of the story and demonstrates to his teacher,
with Anthony's help, his ability to deal with narrative events:

Teacher: '. . . and into the water they fell.'
Anthony: Splash!
Reid: Splash went the boat.
Anthony: It was a big boat that was. He shouldn't let them in.
Teacher: I hope they could all swim.
Anthony: I think so.
Reid: The cat won't be able to.
Teacher: Won't it?
Reid: No.
Anthony: Cats can't swim.
Teacher: Can't they? I don't think pigs can swim either.

Reid is learning about learning as he shares this book with
Anthony and his teacher. He discovers that the information he
needs to help him make sense of the story is not there in the book
and must instead be taken from his own life and knowledge of the
way the world works. He needs to know about floating and sinking,
about deep and shallow water, about the fear of drowning; he also
needs to know about common sense and wisdom and fair play in
order to be able to read the story with any real understanding. The
kind of conversation Reid has here with his teacher is similar to the
conversations he is familiar with at home when he shares a book
with his parents. When Mr Gumpy's boat tips up it triggers a memory of canoeing – and perhaps of being a little afraid of the water:

Teacher: Perhaps the water won't be too deep. Perhaps their feet
will reach the bottom.
Reid: The other day I went to a swimming baths and I had a
seat in a canoe boat with me and I went in a massive . . . I
went in first the children's boat then mummy and
daddy's boat and there was a deep end and a little end.
Teacher: A deep end and a shallow end was it?
Reid: And we taked the boat into the other one then I . . . I went
on my own.

Teacher: Did you?
Reid: But I had to have someone with me. That was my Liam.
Teacher: And he helped look after you. Made sure you were safe
   ... they needed somebody to look after them, didn't they,
   in the story?

Reid's teacher gives him the opportunity of reflecting on the central idea of the story. She knows that the meaning of the book does not lie in its pages, but needs to be remade by Reid himself, with her help. And because of the way she interacts with him he knows this too. Later, as he begins to read independently, he will be able to use this model of learning for himself; in his independent silent reading he will have conversations in his head about ideas and experiences from his world knowledge and from his own life. In the meantime his teacher mediates this learning in her role as an attentive and careful listener, and she helps both children to respond to the story by taking account of their comments and suggestions. In this particular reading she makes no attempt to ask Reid to learn individual words in the story, though she does attend to word meanings by responding to his question about 'bleeding' and suggesting the use of 'shallow' in place of 'little'. But there are significant reading lessons here, and the teacher knows that the children's interest in reading individual words and learning about initial sounds of the alphabet will develop alongside their enjoyment and growing understanding of books.

Six months after starting school, Reid and Helen, also aged 4½, read some of Michael Rosen's poems together from *You Can't Catch Me* (1981). Reid's teacher has read a good many poems to the class this year, and the children know some of them well. Reid has always liked funny poems. Before he came to school he used to ask his father to read Spike Milligan's *Silly Verse for Kids* (1968), and now he is at school Michael Rosen is a favourite with the class. The children know some of his poems by heart. Here, Reid and Helen sit together and decide which poem they will read; this act of choosing is itself a significant feature of the early reading process, because it involves young readers in making their own decisions, and helps them to have a commitment to the text:

Reid: I'll have that one.
Helen: [leafing through the pages] What about 'Jo-Jo'? ... I've had
   that one ... I don't know that one, do you?
Reid: No.
Helen: Do you know that one or that one?

Eventually they opt for 'Down behind the dustbin' and Reid begins to read aloud. Helen interrupts him when he reads 'Jim' instead of 'Sid'. She knows it's wrong:

Reid: 'Down behind the dustbin
        I met a dog called Jim
        He said he didn't know me –'
Helen: Not Jim. Sid.

Reid isn't used to being corrected like this. Normally the adults who read with him accept his version of the story as long as it makes sense. But Helen has a memory of the rhyme in her head and wants it to be exactly right. Reid asks her for clarification. 'What?' he says, 'I can't hear what you're saying.' Helen recites the correct version:

Helen: 'Down behind the dustbin
        I met a dog called Sid,
        He said he didn't know me
        But I said he surely did.'

Reid has now heard the rhyme read correctly and he is prepared to have a go, even though Helen is still a little forceful. He has another go, but falters at the word 'Sid'. Helen tells him again, but perhaps her assertiveness and insistence on accuracy have upset him. Certainly, his reading seems to have lost some of its momentum:

Reid: 'Down behind the dustbin
        I met a dog called . . .'
Helen: Sid.
Reid: Sid. I said he . . . he said he . . .'
Helen: 'He didn't know *me*'
Reid: *me*
Helen: 'But I said he –'
Reid: '*surely did.*'
Helen: '*surely did.*'

If Helen were an adult I would consider her approach to be rather heavy-handed, but she is not an adult and this rhyme (to her mind) has to be correct. The relationship between the two children is not the same as a relationship between an adult and a child, though in this case, Reid has things he could probably learn from Helen.

Reid arrived at school with an understanding of narrative; now in the classroom he often makes up his own complex stories as he draws (Figure 5.1), creating an imaginary world in his head and

Figure 5.1

using it to reflect on his own life by shaping and giving some sort of meaning to his experience:

> One day this policeman saw naughty people being naughty. Then they went to get them. He's very sad 'cos he didn't want to go to jail 'cos he was sorry to be naughty. The policeman said to the little boy, 'You shouldn't have done that.' Because then the light was flashing. He switched the light on 'cos it was getting dark. Then before it was night time I had a biscuit and a drink. Then they lived happily ever after. And that's the end.

Reid knows about the literary conventions of storytelling and he weaves an intricate tale, with the expectation of judgement for wrongdoing coupled with the sense of a happy ending. Events such as these have never actually happened to Reid, yet the feelings they generate – a sense of guilt at doing wrong, fear of retribution and finally the need for comfort and warmth – are there deep inside him and need to be explored in the safety of a story. Perhaps Reid uses this story to give him a way of examining and accepting blame and retribution for something he has done wrong, finally making things all right again in the story through the symbolic comfort of food. I am reminded of Max's journey through his emotions in *Where the Wild Things Are* (1970) and marvel at Sendak's ability to encapsulate children's emotional trials in this extraordinary story. These same emotions are powerful for Reid, and it comes as no surprise to find that a month later he is once again exploring similar feelings through a story he creates while he is drawing. He sat at his table and drew a car again (Figure 5.2) saying: 'This is a different story about that boy who gets lost, but there's going to be a different thing on it.' And this is the story he told as he drew:

Figure 5.2

One day the car when it was green the car just went and the people got run over by an ambulance. The ambulance stopped quickly because there was a car coming. Then they was pretending let's creep out. Now they went into a shop where there was cakes and they smashed the window and they ate one without paying. Then the police came and got the money and took them to jail. Then you could say then the policeman took the cake out of them and put it back in the cake shop.

These two stories are about growing up, balancing that yearning for independence, with its accompanying fears of getting lost and going astray, against the need for the warmth and safety of the known. Reid is using narrative in his stories to reshape and come to terms with events in his own life where he may have been naughty and felt guilt, and he matches this experience against the story of the people who have broken the law, with the policeman representing the authority figure. Reid, operating as a skilled narrator, has crafted these stories in a way which allows him to work out an ethical code for himself.

By the end of his second term in school Reid has taken 20 books home to read. Most are story books, one is a book of poems and one is an information book about making an indoor garden. He has followed his own inclination in his choices and expects each text to make sense to him, evidence perhaps of his growing confidence in himself as a reader.

• • •

Two years later Reid chooses his own books from the library once a month, though his mother steps in to guide him if he chooses books that are far too hard. She says he's very interested in books with photographs in, books about everyday things like going shopping, and dual-language books about Asian children (this is probably because he has been learning Punjabi at school). Recently he has begun choosing books about diving and says he wants to be a diver when he grows up – he watches anything on television to do with diving. Reid has a comic each week and he also enjoys 'books that do things', like pop-up books. He owns two books in a question-and-answer book series about myths and legends and birds and butterflies and he uses these to help him when the family does quizzes together – he is particularly knowledgeable about nature quizzes. His parents says he still loves Raymond Briggs's *The*

Snowman (1978) and likes to listen to the tape of the story set to music.

Reid idolizes Michael Jackson and enjoys his *Moonwalker* (1988) book. 'He has a go at quite difficult words', his mother explains, though she notices that at other times he uses the illustrations to help him sort out the meaning. At school he often uses picture cues too and 'tries to sound out difficult words' – he finds this strategy particularly helpful. He reads in bursts, both at home and at school; sometimes he's very interested in a book but at other times his mother notices that he 'can't be bothered' reading. He still has a bedtime story but these days, instead of being read to all the time by his father, they share the reading more; and sometimes he sits down and reads to himself while he waits for his father to come to his bedroom. 'He whispers the words aloud', his father observes.

Reid is a confident writer and uses his phonological knowledge to help him with spellings. His mother worries about his mirror-writing and wonders if it is because he is left-handed. He recently sat down at home and wrote a long letter to a little girl he is fond of. She used to be in his class but has now left the area.

Part 2

FURTHER

CONSIDERATIONS

6

LEARNING

TO READ

It seems that people would prefer reading to be simple: a simple and easily definable activity with simple ways of learning how to do it. But reading is not a simple activity; it is one of the mind's most complex accomplishments.

(Myra Barrs and Anne Thomas 1991: 2)

The reading biographies in the previous chapters have described five young children who are at the beginning of their reading lives at home and at school. These children already display a complex range of features in their literacy development; this chapter focuses on their knowledge and experience of reading and discusses their impressive range of literacy learning. The children still need the support of an experienced adult reader and will continue to do so for some years; even so, their early knowledge of the reading process shows that they are beginning to do a great many things experienced readers do, but in the manner of a 4-year-old. If they were to be assessed against the National Curriculum level descriptions it is likely that they would all come into the category of 'working towards' Level 1 in terms of their reading competence. Level 1 states that:

Pupils recognise familiar words in simple texts. They use their knowledge of letters and sound-symbol relationships in order to read words and to establish meaning when reading aloud. In these activities they sometimes require support.

> They express their response to poems, stories and non-fiction
> by identifying aspects they like.
>   (Department for Education 1995: 19)

This is probably an accurate summary of the children's development as readers so far but, since the National Curriculum Level
description is couched in very general terms, it can tell us little
about how that reading development happened and nothing at all
about each child as an individual learner. The reading biographies
of the five children are much more detailed and valuable as assessment records because they make a narrative of their early literacy
experiences. When we read them we can begin to see each child's
own learning style emerging, as well as each one's personal reading journey framed by the child's own social and cultural context.
While keeping in mind each child's own unique pathway into reading I intend to focus on some general characteristics of their reading development – with two purposes in mind. First, I want to
ensure that their emergent knowledge about reading is recorded,
caught on the wing as it were. Some of this knowledge is fleeting
and fragmentary and can be easily be overlooked or discounted,
especially if we have not been taught to look for it and identify it as
a positive step on the road to reading. Secondly, teachers and parents who are able to recognize these early competencies and use
them for initial reading assessment will be able to take a wider
view of what the process of becoming a reader entails. The observations of the children's early reading activities show that collectively they are developing their knowledge in five key areas:

They know that print carries a message and that they can gain informa-
tion by reading visual clues as well as text.
Learning to read is crucially about the development of ideas and
concepts, as well as being a linguistic activity. Each time these
young readers were presented with a poem or a story they immediately began to get to grips with its meaning, responding to events
that held their interest and captured their imaginations in ways
that pleased and satisfied them. Typically, they did this by making
connections between the story world and their own lives. They
talked about things that had happened to them when their memory was triggered by characters and events in stories; the opportunity to embed personal stories inside stories from the book world
helped them to understand how book characters feel when they
are in difficult situations. This understanding almost certainly gave

the children the same kind of emotional and intellectual satisfaction that adults get when they read demanding literature.

When Anthony read *Mr Gumpy's Outing* (1970) with his teacher he was demonstrating a humane involvement with the text. He needed no invitation to explore the issues, and his insightful comment 'It was a big boat that was. He shouldn't have let them in' (p. 61) adds to the information given in the text and suggests that he was even meeting some of the requirements of a Level 2 reader by expressing 'opinions about major events or ideas' in the story (Department for Education 1995: 19). Anthony was absorbed and fascinated by the book and was able to detach himself from the events, stepping outside the text to evaluate what Mr Gumpy had done. D. W. Harding suggests that evaluation of characters and events is a central psychological activity on the part of the reader, who not only shares in the events of a story but also reacts *to* a character's behaviour as much as *with* them. Harding (1967: 7) goes on to suggest that it is only in 'successful fiction' that the reader is encouraged to behave in this way, and calls our attention to the kinds of books we put into children's hands – a point that will be considered more fully in the next chapter. The act of becoming a critical reader might appear to be beyond inexperienced child learners; nevertheless, this little boy showed that with encouragement young children are able to use their minds and emotions to help them make sense of stories and, perhaps even more crucially, to carry this learning forward into their personal lives, meeting their own emotional and intellectual needs.

They understand the structure of English grammar, including the structure of stories, and use this knowledge to help them to predict key phrases and sentences and to memorize chunks of 'book language'.

The studies of the five children show how much they already understood about the structure of literary language, a form of language that is markedly different from the kind they use in normal everyday conversations at home and at school. They had begun to understand, even without being consciously taught, that the language used in books is a special kind of language with its own structure and rhythm, often verging on the poetic. As the children absorbed literary language into their own reading patterns they began to read with a 'book voice'. This development is not uncommon in young children who have been sensitized to the language of books. When Carol Fox (1993) analysed the storytelling patterns of the pre-school children in her study, she discovered that they were capable of telling lengthy made-up stories using literary language copied from books or modelled on the storytelling patterns of significant adults. Gemma used this kind of language to retell her version of Goldilocks and the three bears: 'Porridge was too hot and they set off out in the woods' (p. 44). At the same time she displayed her growing sense of story structure by using language to describe the passing of time – 'long time ago'. When Anthony narrated his own version of Little Red Riding Hood he included this use of literary language: 'Once upon a time', 'and he hurried on', 'gobbled her up in one mouthful' (p. 58); all literacy phrases lifted from his textual memory.

As you read the children's reading biographies you might have been aware that I made use of terms borrowed from the language of music. This was quite deliberate and has a bearing on children's adoption of literacy language for their own reading purposes. Words like 'rhythm', 'tune' and 'musicality' are familiar to reading teachers who set out to explain why it is that children seem to respond so readily to texts with patterned and pleasing features. Indeed, intonation in speech has been described by one linguist as its 'melody' and 'music' (Crystal 1987: 173), while Myra Barrs (1992: 16–28) in her essay 'The Tune on the Page' draws attention to the way a text *sounds*, arguing that rhythmic and intonational patterns of language underpin both a story itself and the words of that story. In children's texts this melody or tune is carried in the author's words or tone of voice, mediated for beginning readers by the adult who takes on the role that Marilyn Cochran-Smith (1986: 44) calls 'spokesperson for the text', translating 'from the written to the oral channel'. The teacher who read *Mr Gumpy's Outing* (Burningham 1970) with Reid and Anthony showed them how to 'hear' the tune of that book. Her interpretation of the animals' pleadings: 'May I come please Mr Gumpy?' is both lilting and questioning. Reid and Anthony, joining in with the reading from time to time, learn to read with their ears as they listen and then take over the reading from her, and they too read with expression.

Anthony was aware of the rhythms of written language long before he came to school. His mother had educated him by reading darkly and expressively: '"As long as I live," said Little Red Riding Hood, "I shall never leave the forest path when you have warned me not to do so"' (p. 56). Gurdeep's flamboyant retelling of *Where the Wild Things Are* and his vivacious imitation of the Wild Things' anger (which of course is not obvious from a transcript) indicate that he was using his knowledge of the rhythm of the prose to heighten his performance: 'They gnashed their terrible . . . gnashed they gnashed their terrible . . . ter . . . eyes,' he almost shouted, presumably 'hearing' and anticipating the sounds and rhythms of Sendak's words in his head (p. 33). Percy Scholes (1991: 074), the author of the famous music dictionary, writes of 'the imaginary metronome that seems to form part of the mental equipment of every human being', and there is no doubt that Gurdeep was secure enough inside Sendak's rhythm to let himself go, experiencing the pleasure of playing with whole chunks of text, probably 'feeling' the rhythm in his head.

In both linguistics and music, rhythm is made up of several distinct features: young readers have to understand how to interpret all these components as they 'play' the text of a book. Rhythm is made up of:

Stress – the accented syllables

Pitch – the rise and fall of the tune or the voice (Listen to yourself reading 'and he sailed off through night and day and in and out of weeks and almost over a year to where the Wild Things are'. Where do you hear your voice going higher or lower?)

Dynamics – the loudness or softness of the sound (How do you read the final page of *Where the Wild Things Are* ['and it was still hot'] – loudly or softly?)

Tempo – the pace of the delivery (How do you think Anthony read, 'Went rumpeta, rumpeta, rumpeta all the way down the road' – fast or slow, and why? [p. 62])

Colour – the timbre of the instrument or human voice. This is difficult to show on paper but perhaps one of the clearest examples is Gemma and Geeta's retelling of the story of Goldilocks and the three bears. The girls set off together on a journey through the book, intertwining their voices which are alternately deep and rather softly-pitched, making the whole business work for them by listening to each other (p. 45):

Geeta: She she sitting in baby chair and she crashed. Really sorry. She sitting . . .

Gemma: I know it. She went upstairs and she tries daddy's bed. Too high. Tried mummy's bed. Too high. Tried mummy's bed. Too . . .

Geeta: Lumpy.

Gemma: Lumpy. Tries baby bear's bed. Just right.

The most significant aspect of these rhythmic features, in both music and language, is their support in keeping the momentum going. When children learn to read, the only way they can learn the tune of the text is by listening to an experienced reader doing it for them, and then being encouraged to have a go for themselves. No amount of knowledge of sight vocabulary or phonic awareness will give children the skill to tackle this interpretation of textual voice. They have to hear how it goes on the page, over and over again. And as each encounter with a new text, and a new author, will be different, the child has to tune into the stress, pitch, colour, dynamics and tempo of each story, interpreted for them by the reading teacher who becomes the storyteller on the author's behalf.

But what happens to the rhythmic quality of reading in the case of young emergent bilingual readers whose first language does not correspond to the stress patterns of English? Gurdeep and Geeta are both Punjabi-speaking, and Carolyn Steedman has this to say about the timing of Punjabi:

> Punjabi has a very strong tendency towards syllable timing. The poetic system of Punjabi represents in a heightened form the halfway position that it occupies as a language along the continuum of syllable-timed/stress-timed world languages. Punjabi poetry involves the combination and patterning of long and short syllables, and is in this way unlike, for example, the poetry of an extremely syllable-timed language like French, where it is the absolute number of syllables that makes a poetic unit.
>
> (Steedman 1992: 99)

It seems appropriate to incorporate some of Steedman's evidence here. Some years ago she wrote about a girl she taught called Amarjit, a 9-year-old Punjabi speaker. She describes how Amarjit adapted a story she had grown fond of in a book written in English and made up her own song, setting the English words of the story to a tune that seems to have been drawn from her own Punjabi tradition. 'She sustained the melody over a considerable portion of the book,' writes Steedman (1992: 92) 'and with some skill dealt with the difficulties of incorporating the irregular rhythms of prose in regular melody.' This activity was possibly made easier for her because in Punjabi, poetry is a medium of instruction, and what is apparent from Steedman's observation is that Amarjit had done a great of deal of learning by heart, something children in English primary schools are not expected to do to any great extent. Amarjit's knowledge of Punjabi, and the musical system based on

Punjabi, seems to have helped her to relate the phonological system of this language to her learning of the timing and intonation
patterns of English. It is possible that Amarjit sang hymns and
accompanied herself on the harmonium at home or at the temple
or knew folk songs or children's songs from her own culture. If she
did she might have been able to set the words of the English text to
a tune with a regular rhythm that she was already familiar with.
There is certainly room for whole areas of enquiry into this kind of
learning. I still have little idea of how Gurdeep and Geeta took on
the stress timing of English when they read literary texts in their
second language.

What emerges from this discussion is that the reading aloud of
texts – stories, poems, songs, over and over again – must form a key
part of the teaching and learning of reading. The experienced
adult – either teacher or parent – who 'models' the language of
books for children is doing something vitally important because
children will imitate the uses of language they hear. Gurdeep's
teacher knew this when she helped him to understand the 'voice
on the page' and to use it for himself when he tried to recall the
patterns and rhythms of *Where the Wild Things Are* (Sendak 1970),
memorizing 'chunks' of the text in his own retelling as he
attempted to master the language of the book. He knew the words
of the story could not be changed – another crucial reading lesson
– and, driven by the need to get them right, to make them sound
the way he knew they ought to go, he practised over and over
again. All the time he was getting closer to Sendak's language,
making the words have a special sound and rhythm of their own
and discovering what Margaret Meek (1982: 22) calls 'the tune on
the page'.

*They know how to handle books and they understand the conventions of
print – turning pages from left to right, turning back to reread a particular
section or to check on an illustration from a previous page.*
All five children were learning where to open a book up, where the
story began and where to turn a page, coordinating hand and eye
movements across the page and orienting from left to right.
Children who have their books held for them and their pages
turned for them may be slower to learn some aspects of these
important processes. The children in this study were also learning,
with the help of their teachers, to direct their gaze *around* a page so
that the text and illustrations worked together to help the story
unfold – and good writers, illustrators and editors work to make

this task easier. When Anthony looked at a book and asked his teacher, 'Is this the beginning?' (p. 60), he was demonstrating to her that he knew about the structure of a story – that it has a beginning and an end – but he wasn't sure how to relate this knowledge to the way beginnings and endings are presented in books.

Though most books in the English tradition follow the conventional left-to-right sequencing – and children need to know this – it's worth remembering that some forms of print that children are in daily contact with do not follow a simple left-to-right convention and may even present words in a totally different format. (Gurdeep was fascinated by coins, requiring him to read round the edge in a circular fashion, and by bank notes, with their many different writing layouts.) Many children frequently see parents writing lists from top to bottom of a piece of paper and see newspapers set out in columns, with headlines. (Gemma watched her father doing the crossword, writing words from top to bottom as well as from left to right.) And in many towns and cities children meet the word 'Ambulance' on the front of the vehicle written not only right to left but with the letters laterally inverted. These are complex reading lessons indeed: some of them can be rehearsed in the classroom home corner, on posters and wall charts, in home-made books and in notices placed strategically around the classroom.

They are becoming familiar with metalanguage – the language to talk about language, such as 'word', 'sentence', 'letter', 'title', 'page', 'cover'. The children had learned that there is a special language in which you can talk about language. Many reading teachers take it for granted – but should we? – that beginning readers are familiar with terms like 'read', 'write', 'draw' and 'talk' when they come to school. When young children share books with adults they often become aware that there are special words they can use when they want to talk about language, and reading a story together is an obvious context in which to introduce and discuss this specialized language, pointing to a 'word', a 'letter' or a whole 'sentence' as appropriate in the text.

They are learning about the correspondence between letters and sounds and are beginning to discriminate between letter-shapes. They are also learning to recognize individual words.
This particular linguistic feature of reading development is most pronounced in Geeta's early reading, and she is certainly

extremely conscious of words, letters and sounds. This might be because she is learning to read in her second language, and one huge advantage held by emergent bilingual readers seems to be their ability to understand that objects can be separated from the labels that stand for them. Eve Gregory (1996: 51), in her detailed study of emergent bilingual learners, identified their 'advanced metalinguistic and analytic awareness' as among the most pronounced reading behaviours in their reading repertoire. Young children obviously need to learn about the connection between sounds and letters – the 'phonological awareness' of the programmes of study for reading (Department for Education 1995: 7). This teaching can be done, as Geeta's teacher has shown, by direct reference to a book (p. 81) but this particular form of reading knowledge can also be taught directly, through rhymes and jingles and alphabet games, where children are introduced to written symbols and sounds. Many teachers play games like I-Spy to introduce initial sounds, and also invent rhymes for children to join in with based on alliteration. Most usefully, children can use their knowledge of sounds and letters when they are engaged in their own writing, learning to spell for the first time. Home-made books can provide an excellent support for introducing the alphabet, where children learn to recognize upper- and lowercase letters, letter names and sounds, and alphabetical order (see discussion on 'The Delicious Alphabet' below).

The process of learning to recognize one's own name and to represent it in writing is an important early stage in literacy development. The five children were all very interested in the way their own names were represented on paper and that their names were permanent markers. (Gemma's name remained on her birthday cards even when she put them away and closed the drawer (see p. 39).) The learning of one's name is powerful and symbolic. Children develop a personal awareness about language and its uses when they see themselves represented in print and learn to write their names.

Young children's knowledge of various forms of print they see around them in the environment is a further indication of a personal interest in language and reading. Their ability to differentiate between Weetabix and Cocopops, or to recognize when *Jaws* or the Transformers or Care Bears are on the television, presents children with new and demanding reading tasks for which there is high motivation. Collectively and impressively, the children's pre-school knowledge of public forms of print took in the following areas:

food labels, newspapers, shopping catalogues, calendars (in English and Punjabi), advertisements (in brochures, catalogues and on television), birthday cards, wedding invitations (in English and Punjabi), letters, bills, crosswords, the writing on coins and bank notes, pools coupons, lists, diet sheets, tickets, appointment cards, number plates and maps. This wide variety of public print offers enormous scope for extending reading knowledge at home; at school and in the classroom various forms of public print can be used in rewarding ways to increase children's knowledge of literacy. Margaret Meek has this to say about the value of this form of print:

> Public print has an important place in the lives of many young children before they come to school because it is interwoven in the daily transactions with family and community. Many a non-reader has failed just because he did not link the way he looked at advertisements on his way to school with what he has to look at on the school notice board. It is so easy for us to take all public print for granted that we often forget our part in pointing it out as something to be looked at. One of the paradoxes of being literate as that we know so well what notices and signs are, and what they say, that we no longer look at them. The learner, on the other hand, can make good use of such things.
>
> (Meek 1982: 41)

An example is in order. Ann Ketch, a teacher in an inner-city school in the West Midlands, realized that children were coming into her class with a great deal of experience of some forms of public print. She took advantage of their knowledge of food labels by developing a special alphabet book for them to read based on various sweets, drinks and savouries they often brought to school for lunch. She photographed the wrappers or labels on 26 different brands of food or drink that the children were familiar with, arranged the photographs in alphabetical order, and made them up into a book, alluringly entitled 'The Delicious Alphabet' (Ketch 1991). The wrappings represented the initial sounds of each product from A through to Z (though Z proved difficult):

> Aero, Boost, diet Coke, Double Decker, Eclairs, Flake, Galaxy, Hula Hoops, Ice Breaker, Jump, Kitkat, Lion, Mars, Novo, Opal Fruits, Polo, Quaver, Rolo, Smarties, Twix, United, diet Vimto, Wispa, XXX Extra Strong Mints, Yorkie, (Smarties were laid out in the form of a letter Z).

Children who are invited to read a book like this can have their attention drawn to different areas of reading knowledge: predicting what the book might be about; making meaning by telling personal stories about individual items of food; handling the book – turning the pages, reading from left to right, and rereading and browsing; learning the names of letters and their initial sounds and identifying upper- and lowercase letters; learning about phonic blends, beginning to understand alphabetical order; observing and talking about different print fonts (italics, joined-up writing, and so on); sight-reading individual words.

• • •

In this chapter I have identified five areas of reading in which the children were beginning to show some competence: making meaning from texts; understanding the structure of language; handling books; developing an awareness of metalanguage; learning about letters and sounds and recognizing individual words. As their competence increases they will have to learn something even more complex; they will need to know which particular area or areas of knowledge they need to call upon in order to read efficiently. Should they be prepared to guess – to keep the flow going – or do they need to be absolutely accurate? Do they need to slow the pace of their reading right down in order to unpick each word carefully for a special purpose? Some of our finest research into early reading insists that the major role of the teacher lies in helping children to 'orchestrate' this vital skill of deciding how to read a certain text. I have borrowed this term from Anne Bussis and her colleagues (1985: 114) who carried out a major piece of classroom-based research into reading, working with 40 children from inner-city schools. They described and analysed the children's individual learning styles in meticulous detail. One of their most important conclusions was that efficient reading demands an orchestration of the forward momentum – keeping the reading going – and the accuracy needed in order to be faithful to the writer's meaning. By implication then, the sensitive reading teacher will always try to help children to balance the mastery of meaning with word accuracy. This is possibly the hardest lesson of all for young readers. Henrietta Dombey gives us a clue about how they should go about doing this when she reminds us that:

> No one source of information – phonics, spelling patterns, syntactic, semantic, textual or picture cues – can provide the

reader with the means for fluent and accurate word identifi-
cation, or with a valid and satisfying conception of the meaning of the text. Children need to learn how to make smooth
and simultaneous use of all sources of information. This can
only develop as they focus on building a coherent meaning
from the words and pictures in front of them.

(Dombey 1992: 15)

Making sense of the text – 'building a coherent meaning' – is what
is central to this reading activity, and it requires children to be
reflective about their reading. This process of reflection is already
happening for Reid and Geeta, who are making statements about
themselves as learners: 'Amber shows me how I can read. How I
can really read so I can do the words' (p. 93); 'The Snowman
haven't got words. Just have to get some words' (p. 74). It is part of
the teacher's role to help these children become even more aware
of what they are doing when they read, extending their reflective
ability to the act of reading itself, so that they read and at the same
time observe themselves reading.

Many of the examples I have used in this chapter are taken from
the children's reading of story books, and this is no coincidence.
Stories – the ones they invent for themselves and those they discover in books – are crucially important for children in supporting
their early reading development. The kinds of books they read and
the relationship between the language in those books and the
beginning of reading will be the subject of the next chapter.

7

THE ROLE OF

STORY IN YOUNG

CHILDREN'S LIVES

My argument is that narrative, like lyric or dance, is not to be
regarded as an aesthetic convention used by artists to control,
but as a primary act of mind transferred from art to life.

(Barbara Hardy 1977: 12)

In the last chapter I discussed the kinds of reading knowledge that
Gurdeep, Gemma, Anthony, Geeta and Reid were developing in
their first encounters with print. I suggested that their range of
reading knowledge is impressive in its complexity. This chapter
extends the discussion of the characteristics of children's early
reading development by exploring the place of story in their reading lives – the wild and zany stories they invent for themselves in
their play, the collection of stories they tell themselves about their
own lives, the stories they hear from those around them; and, of
course, the stories they meet in books, ranging from the simple
to the humorous, the curious to the downright subversive. This
chapter raises issues about the role of story in early reading and
discusses how children's intrinsic need for stories enables them to
put their own lives in order. Three key arguments underpin the
discussion. First, that books and stories help young children to
explore their own experience and to make connections back to the
world of the book. Secondly, that illustrations in picture books can
promote young's children's interest in visual forms of literacy and

help them to read printed text. Thirdly, that picture books help young readers to gain a mastery over different forms of reading knowledge.

I want now to dwell a little on some theoretical considerations about the place of narrative in people's lives. The quotation from Barbara Hardy at the head of this chapter reminds us that narrative is a 'primary act of mind': it is a natural and normal human process. Harold Rosen, in *Stories and Meanings* (c. 1984: 14–15) argues too that 'our human bent for narratizing experience' is fundamental to the human species. He adds: 'The simplest narrative which would seem to be a report of recent events (yesterday's quarrel, losing and finding the front-door key, buying a suit) is itself an invention, an act of imagination.' All people in all cultures weave their experience into stories, using language to shape their day-to-day experiences. When we enter a narrative world we select and reshape events in our lives through our dreams and daydreams, through our gossip with friends and neighbours; and, if we are young children, we tell ourselves stories before we go to sleep. Ruth Weir (1970) demonstrated this when she documented the pre-sleep monologues of her son, Anthony. Her tape recordings reveal that between the ages of 2 years 4 months and 2 years 6 months, while he talked himself to sleep every night, he was having conversations with 'companions' and entering an imaginary world as he did so.

Teachers and parents who watch young children at play in the back garden at home or in the playground at school know they have no difficulty in stepping outside their own lives and entering a world of the imagination. That this is a creative process involving enormous outpourings of emotional energy, intelligence, self-discipline and single-mindedness is perhaps less obvious. Anthony had no trouble creating and maintaining a world he invented for himself as he played with his Lego: 'Mine can change into something else', he told his friend, as he transformed his Lego model (p. 58). There can be no doubting his enormous excitement and commitment as he released himself from the powerlessness of his childhood state into a make-believe world where he was fully in control of his own destiny and able to make things happen. He used his facility with language to manipulate and restructure his experience, representing the world to himself and his friend in new ways. We are familiar too with the vigour with which children play in the home corner, and it was there that Geeta enacted the roles that took her into imaginary territory. She explored possible futures and, just for a few moments, she ran her own household. As a member of a close family, this rehearsal for adulthood and family life helped Geeta to learn something of her family structure by acting out the role of responsible mother and sister (p. 73). Anthony (p. 38) and Geeta (p. 73) used props like Lego, dolls, a toy dog, and so on alongside their talk to help them invent and act out their stories; but children don't necessarily need toys to help them to do this. The five children often showed how skilled they were when they created new scenarios through their drawings and their accompanying monologues, inventing a world of 'let's pretend' on paper, often *drawing the action* as they told their stories and shaping their imaginary worlds through their language. Marian Whitehead describes the process like this:

> Being able to think about people, animals, objects and experiences in their absence means that, in a special way, we still have a hold on them. The hold is special because it is created mentally and is not totally subject to reality or present facts. Furthermore, we can experiment with these representations: we can play and pretend with them. Young children, from at least the second year of life, can say 'miaow' like a cat, or climb into the cat's basket and curl up to sleep.
>
> (Whitehead 1990: 144)

When Anthony told the story of *Jaws* and drew his pictures of the action he was exploring some of the violent confrontations in the film version of the text, and by writing himself in as centre-stage star he shifted the medium from video film to his own personal and oral retelling of the story. There is no doubt that he was totally engrossed in this imaginative task, and with enormous skill and energy he managed to intertwine his imaginary life experiences within his intertextual borrowings from the screen version of the story (p. 64). Gurdeep's instinctive narrative response to the photographs in his album grew out of his human need to give some sort of shape to his life, to talk about the past and the future and possibly to prepare himself for the life he will live (p. 24).

When children explore a world of their imagination away from their day-to-day lives, they are doing something so clever, yet so subtle, that we often overlook its significance. When Gurdeep read *Where the Wild Things Are* (Sendak 1970) he was able to leave behind the immediate situation of the classroom and enter voluntarily into a world of ideas and exotic travel, and as he followed Max on his journey he was at the same time developing abstract thought processes (p. 33–4). Gordon Wells's significant research into the development of children's language at home and at school (1981, 1985, 1987) highlights the role of story in developing their abstract thought processes. When he checked back on the pre-school learning experiences of children who took part in his long-term study and who were successful in Knowledge of Literacy tests at the ages of 7 and 11, he found that they could all be positively identified by one feature: they were the ones who had had stories told or read to them before they came to school. But why stories particularly? Why not other activities? Wells hypothesizes that in the act of understanding the story world, children are pushed towards the use of decontextualized language and have to make meaning using words alone. It is this sustained activity of making a world in the head that calls for higher levels of cognitive thought. In the act of listening to stories:

> the child is beginning to come to grips with the symbolic potential of language, its power to represent experience in symbols which are independent of the objects, events and relationships which are symbolised, and which can be interpreted in contexts other than those in which the experience originally occurred.
>
> (Wells 1985:134)

Wells's evidence led him to hypothesize that stories have a role in children's wider learning that goes far beyond their contribution to their entertainment, or the teaching of reading, writing and literature, because in order to understand a story a child has to pay careful attention to symbolic language to be able to get at the meaning. Simply, this calls for higher levels of cognitive thinking. Stories make people intelligent.

When Anthony told his teacher that Mr Gumpy 'shouldn't have let them in' (p. 61) he had made a profound leap away from his everyday surroundings and entered an imaginary world made solely through the pages of a book. Like all children who deal with symbolic meanings he was working at the high cognitive level suggested by Wells, interpreting the author's language and overlaying it with meaning. Similarly, when Anthony's teacher read *The Elephant and the Bad Baby* (Vipont 1969) Anthony could of course not look around the classroom for any clues about the meaning of this story – there were no elephants or babies there to help him make sense of it. Instead, he had to work hard to reconstruct Elvira Vipont's words for himself, using his own knowledge of elephants and babies and what it means to be 'bad'. We know he has done this successfully when he goes on to tell his own version of the story, beginning, 'Once there was an elephant . . .' (p. 62).

It may appear that this discussion has very little to do with the process of learning to read, but as we reflect on the similarities between the play world of the small child and the narrative world created by an author, we can begin to understand that it is a small step to introduce the notion of the story book into children's familiar world of make-believe play and storytelling. Many young children, just like those in this book, are experienced in handling different kinds of narrative before they come to school. Jill, a 5-year-old girl in Carol Fox's study (1983: 17), became the 'broadcaster-storyteller' of the text she made up, experimenting with sound effects and songs and using what Fox calls 'a range of voices' to take on the roles of two broadcasters (each with a different part), the storyteller, and various characters in her story. The complexity of her self-appointed task leaves us reeling. We can be similarly amazed that children confidently explore complex human themes like birth and death, illness, anger, punishment, family relationships, the past and the future in some of their most commonplace oral stories. In Fox's continuing research (1989: 26) into the oral story monologues of pre-school children, 5-year-old Josh narrates a lengthy story in three chapters set in heaven, where he plays God, St Peter, Dracula, Frankenstein, a puppy, a dragon and a host of heavenly servants. Fox shows how Josh and other young children told stories which 'reveal[ed] that they [were] not only familiar with the ways stories get told, in books and out of them, but that they [were] also familiar with the texts of the social and physical realities they encounter[ed] every day'. The only possible response to this powerful and significant storying is to make sure that the story books we put in children's hands reflect this complexity so that young readers can use them to enter the imaginary world inside the cover to explore new situations and experiences, just as they do in the home corner, or with the Lego or on paper, or through their photograph albums.

As soon as a child opens up a book the author and illustrator draw them into the scene: perhaps it's Max's bedroom, or the river by Mr Gumpy's house, or a deep dark forest. The child risks entering the story world, senses its mood, uses the book as a toy or a prop, 'plays' with it and creates a story from its pages. Without this act of creation on the child's part, there can be no story. *Mr Gumpy's Outing* (Burningham 1970) proved to be a distinctive story for Anthony and Reid (pp. 60–2; 93–5), and it's no coincidence that Victor Watson (1996a: 160) describes this story as 'one of the wisest books ever made for young readers'. Why? Because 'the words and pictures exist in perfect balance; neither demand too much attention'. It's a book that encourages young readers to explore the events and talk in depth about what happens, renegotiating the meaning and generating hypotheses (remember Anthony's 'Cats can't swim' (p. 61)). Books like this encourage what Watson and his colleague Morag Styles (1996: 2) call the 'readerly gap'; they define this as 'that imaginative space that lies hidden somewhere between the words and the pictures, or in the mysterious syntax of the pictures themselves, or between the shifting perspectives and untrustworthy voices of the narratives'. Watson and Styles are identifying the part played by the child who has to collaborate with the author and illustrator to read and shape the narrative.

Stories such as those explored by the children in earlier chapters offer them a chance to explore, in symbolic form, the problems and possibilities involved in inescapable human events. Universal challenges, struggles and physical dangers that exist in the human world resound through the pages of these books, and these themes form the substance of the folk-fairy tales, myths and legends of many cultures, often appearing in the guise of giants, wolves, witches, bears, monsters, or as quests to be undertaken. The conflicts and tensions of growing towards independence and maturity are echoed in the language and illustrations of many picture books, where danger appears in the shape of a fox in *Rosie's Walk* (Hutchins 1968) and anger takes on the form of a Wild Thing in *Where the Wild Things Are* (Sendak 1970) – the book that Margaret Spencer (1976: 20) acclaims as 'one of the most enchanting stories ever told or depicted', explaining that it 'is a symbolic representation of the complicated childhood experience of guilt and restitution'. It is little wonder that some children need to reread a particular story many times, because it contains complex meanings and emotions which they need to explore and hold on to. Authors of good children's fiction are aware of the struggle going on in children's inner lives, and they present their stories in a form that children can understand and respond to. Writers and illustrators like Maurice Sendak, John Burningham, Pat Hutchins, Shirley Hughes, Raymond Briggs, David McKee and Anthony Browne (to name a few) present deep universal experience and emotion in ways children can handle in safety, between the covers of a book.

The importance of having this range of literature in the early years classroom is reflected in the current National Curriculum programmes of study for reading at Key Stage 1 (Department for Education 1995: 6), which state that young readers should have 'an extensive experience of children's literature . . . including stories, poetry, plays and picture books'. These books should have 'interesting subject matter and settings', 'a clear viewpoint', 'use of language that benefits from being read aloud and re-read', and 'language with repetitive patterns, rhyme and rhythm'. Teachers will have to make their own decisions about which books meet these criteria. Some responsible publishers of new reading schemes have taken the initiative and published books that take account of the National Curriculum guidelines. Their books present young children with a wide range of genres and introduce them to authors who understand children's desire for complex, challenging and stimulating texts, with meanings interwoven between picture and words. Moreover, some of these new reading series invite children to browse and reread texts as a matter of course. This has not always been the case. Barrie Wade, in his perceptive analysis of one very traditional reading scheme, draws our attention to a psychological illness that he calls 'reading rickets'. This disease is brought on by 'the potential conflict in the minds of children caused by any reading which promotes arbitrariness instead of pattern, disconnection rather than coherence and emptiness rather than fulfilment' (Wade 1982: 33–4). Wade argues that the repetition of incoherent, meaningless phrases abandons any attempt at literary merit in the blind support of the development of word recognition alone. He is right to make a fuss about books like these because they expose children to the effects of mediocrity.

The awkward phrasing and stilted syntax found in much traditional reading material for beginning readers presents young children with a written style that does not encourage them to use their skill to predict what comes next. With the introduction of stimulating and interesting reading series, let us hope that the media-provoked debate between 'real books' and 'reading schemes', partly inspired by the general poor quality of books in earlier reading series – a residue of which still lines the shelves of our classrooms – can now be placed in its historical context, and that teachers will have the confidence and the necessary finance to introduce texts in their classrooms that match children's narrative sophistication and give them new and challenging reading lessons.

One feature of demanding reading texts for children is their intertextual nature. Earlier in this book we were able to observe Geeta making connections between the three bears in *The Jolly Postman* (Ahlberg and Ahlberg 1986) and the three bears in the Goldilocks story she knew well ('We got three bears of that haven't we?' (p. 75)). We should perhaps not be surprised that many children's stories, both traditional and modern, have overlapping themes nor that children become skilled in carrying meaning from one book to another, and from one medium to another. Children's writers like Janet and Allan Ahlberg deliberately exploit children's knowledge and skill for spotting intertextual links by introducing characters and events into their stories that come straight out of traditional tales. They rely on their young readers' knowledge of well-known stories to make the new story work. Wolfgang Iser (1978: 107) reminds us that reading is never a one-way process from author to reader; rather, it is a dynamic interaction between the reader and the text. It is the reader who must do the work of building images for the story in order to take meaning from it and make connections between the story and everyday life.

Traditional reading schemes such as the one that Barrie Wade analysed were obviously intended to promote children's reading development. Instead, they probably retarded children's reading progress because of their concentration on one or two kinds of reading knowledge – typically a key word sight vocabulary or a concentration on phonic awareness – at the expense of others. These books often contained illustrations that simply echoed rather than extended the ideas in the text. But good children's writers don't tell their readers everything about the story; instead, they invite them to shape the meaning for themselves and they often use the role of illustration for this purpose. Judith Graham (1990: 67) argues that we have underestimated how much illustrations are likely to support the teaching and learning of reading. Pictures, she says, help children to understand the deep meaning of stories, because they show the reader how to find out more about characters and events, and also make it possible for readers to learn about the structure and shape of stories. The National Curriculum programmes of study for reading (Department for Education 1995: 6) stipulate that illustrations in picture books should '*enhance* the words of the text' [my italics]. Images in good children's picture books do this. They enrich and extend the text, often drawing on children's willingness to examine pictures in minute detail. The forms of illustration in children's books –

cartoons, split-page images, realistic or highly symbolic visual themes – lead children's eyes and minds forward, enabling them to get through a book by turning from one picture to the next, one sentence to the next, and one page to the next – though it does not follow that children can 'read' them accurately, as Henrietta Dombey points out:

> Young children do, of course, find pictures easier to read than words. We should neither dismiss this meaning-making activity, nor assume that children are highly skilled in it. They may need more help than we realise in making sense of pictures: a landing-stage can be misread as a table and a second picture of the tiger misread as a second tiger. Intentions, moods and consequences may only become apparent when they are talked about.
>
> (Dombey 1992: 14)

Children are often able to anticipate events because illustrations carry subtle clues about the nature of the story that go unmentioned in the text – for instance, there is a drawing of a Wild Thing at the bottom of Max's staircase in *Where the Wild Things Are* (Sendak 1970) but it is never referred to directly. Children who watch films and videos learn to interrogate moving pictures, 'reading' subtle clues in the form of images on the screen. The vitality of their interrogation of the illustrations in picture books, and their teacher's encouragement to respond to the mood of the illustration, helps them to create the story alongside the author and illustrator.

If we accept the continuing support that stories and picture books offer young children it is clear why Eve Gregory (1996: 78) supports the use of picture books when working with emergent bilingual readers. Some bilingual children can be disadvantaged when they have to understand what particular English words mean (remember Geeta's trouble with the word 'tatty'? (p. 79)). Gregory (1996: 114–17) maintains that stories can help children like Geeta to predict and extend their English vocabulary because the authors of story books set uncommon words in a context the child is often familiar with. These helpful texts give the child a means of making sense of an unknown word and of understanding how it fits into the wider framework of a phrase or sentence. Similarly, Gregory's research confirms that picture books provide emergent bilingual readers with the support for building phonic awareness and for learning about the structure of language

itself. Their familiar and often repeated patterns help these children to predict familiar texts and to approach new books with confidence. For example, picture books like *We're Going on a Bear Hunt*
(Rosen 1989) can be used to introduce children to regular patterns
of letters and sounds through the rhyming text – phrases like the
'swirling, whirling snowstorm' and the 'splash splosh' of the family
wading through the river, give the reading teacher plenty of
opportunities to extend children's awareness of phonemic patterns. Gregory also argues that the contents of picture books can
increase emergent bilingual children's knowledge of the world by
introducing them to new cultural experiences they might not have
met in their own homes. The stories also help these children to
make important links between their own culture and the culture
of the book by embedding new learning inside recognizable and
universal moral values.

Competent and experienced teachers never base their teaching
on oversimplified methodologies. They know that the development of reading is a complex area that involves the teaching and
learning of a great deal of knowledge, and a balancing of that
knowledge and experience. They know too that there will never be
just one kind of text, nor one published teaching method, that will
take over the task of teaching children to read. But what do we do
with the wealth of picture books if we are not simply to read and
enjoy them in that sleepy comfortable half-hour at the end of the
busy school day? I recently worked with a group of teachers to
explore ways of supporting children's early reading with picture
books. In an intense hour we produced a series of excellent
schemes of work using the following headings to direct our thinking about reading experiences offered by the picture book:

Introducing the book	Developing confidence in
Developing phonic awareness	handling books
Exploring issues in the story	Organizing paired or
Developing a sight vocabulary	group work
Encouraging visual literacy	Developing cross-
Encouraging an interest in	curricular links
authorship	Using resources
Encouraging an awareness of	Following on – where
language	next?

In writing these schemes of work we took account of wide
aspects of the reading process and were flexible enough to shift the
learning focus towards either the textual or the pictorial emphasis

of a particular book. The framework of these schemes of work, with the emphasis on many areas of reading experience, acknowledges the interconnectedness of the reading task with the other language modes of talking, listening and writing. Our common starting point in every case was the picture book, and through our schemes children will be encouraged to extend their reading knowledge in areas covering meaning and context, grammar and linguistics, phonological awareness and book-handling.

In this chapter I have argued for the teaching and learning of reading based on story. I have done this because it is through story that children move with unrestrained pleasure between the imaginary world of play to the make-believe world of the book. Young children who have opportunities to talk their way through books can respond to characters and events and find ways of linking the meaning of the story with meanings in their own lives, all at a high intellectual level. Stories, therefore, help children to develop cognitive abilities and to deal with universal emotions and feelings. Most importantly, story books support early reading by their delightful and predictable uses of language. In addition these books offer the reading teacher a way of exploring the patterns of phonemes and individual words that are necessary for reading development. But children cannot understand these things alone. In order to do this learning effectively children need practice in reading collaboratively with others who will help them towards that understanding. The nature of this important relationship will be explored in the next chapter.

8

READING

PARTNERSHIPS

The more likely parents are to give good answers, the more likely are children to ask interesting questions.

(Jerome Bruner 1986: 76)

The reading biographies of the five children cover only a relatively short period of time but even so, the evidence shows that they have already spent an important part of their reading lives in partnership with a more experienced person, usually a parent or teacher and occasionally an older sibling. The reading they did together illustrates how the more experienced reader has been able to foster and maintain a successful reading partnership with the child learner. It is after all the reading teacher who make decisions about what the young reader needs in the way of instruction, who responds to the child's attempts to get a conversation going, and who assesses the child's short- and long-term reading development. This chapter elaborates on these processes and shows how experienced readers can work alongside young children to give them support and encouragement to become more competent and increasingly independent.

Lev Vygotsky (1978: 86) describes this area of teaching and learning as the 'zone of proximal development'. This, he says, represents 'the distance between the actual developmental level as determined by independent problem-solving and the level of potential development as determined through problem-solving under adult guidance or in collaboration with more capable peers'. In other words, the teacher's role lies in knowing how much the child can do, how much support to give, and where the difference lies. Jerome Bruner (cited in Wertsch 1985: 29) expands on Vygotsky's theories and explains that the first thing a person in the teaching role must do is to 'model the task, to establish that something is possible and interesting'. The teacher's second job is to judge when a child has enough confidence to try out the task independently. The technical term used by Bruner to describe this kind of interaction, where the adult first gives full support and then gradually withdraws (though never abandons) that supporting hand, is 'scaffolding'. Bruner defines this as the reduction of 'the number of degrees of freedom that the child must manage in the task'. When this teaching and learning model is applied to the teaching of reading, the experienced reader initially takes responsibility for the whole reading task and then gradually eases off to allow the child to take over more of the reading, while still giving as much support as necessary.

Few of us are born knowing how to help an individual child learn to read and it is a point of considerable satisfaction that the reading partnerships documented in this study are characterized by warm, confident and intelligent reading behaviour on the part of experienced adults who read alongside young children both in school and out. Most notably, perhaps, these teachers appear to make no outward distinction between reading and learning to read. Their aim, whether stated explicitly or not, is to involve each child as much as possible in understanding the author's words, while introducing elements of direct teaching as appropriate. They all, in their own ways, make great play of the child's need to talk about a story and most are willing to give the child time to explore the meaning. So the words of the story often become intertwined with conversational talk; there are regular pauses to laugh at the funny bits, to repeat sections of the text and to talk spontaneously about memories triggered by the story. It is as if the experienced readers observed here know instinctively that talking about incidents in a story and matching them to events in a child's real life can help that child both to understand the text at a deeper and more sophisticated level, and to become a young critic of characters and situations.

We can see several examples of Bruner's 'scaffolding' process at work in the children's biographies. This term describes precisely what Gemma's mother is doing when she first reads *Me in Puddles*

(Wolff 1979) to her daughter and then encourages Gemma towards early independence by asking her to read the story herself. First she gives Gemma the 'model' of how to do it by letting her hear the words of the story read aloud, with the appropriate intonational patterns, sometimes pausing to talk about events: then she encourages Gemma to have a go herself. The problem for the adult reader, sitting alongside the child, book in hand, is always to decide how the book should be tackled. Who will read the book and who will be the listener? Or should the task be shared? How should the pictures be 'read' and understood as part of the story? How to begin – and how to finish? In successful reading partnerships the adult often tells the child the title of the book or, if the child has read the book before, asks if they can remember the title, thus setting the scene for what is to follow. In the most successful encounters the adult is a careful listener, observer, assessor and planner, responding to what the child says and does and encouraging the child to enter the fascinating world of speculation and exploration of ideas and language. Most importantly, the adult's function is never punitive. Worthwhile reading sessions always hold the promise of security and the reward of the story.

Many good features of this kind of interaction with a book occur when Anthony and Reid share with their teacher *Mr Gumpy's Outing* (Burningham 1970) (pp. 60–2; 93–5). In view of the fact that this is such a rich encounter with a book, I want to examine it again here in some detail, but this time with the focus firmly on what the teacher is doing in her supportive role. It's worth noting, though it's not apparent in this silent, imageless transcript, that the teacher is reading with an expressive and almost musically rich voice, and when the children join in they echo the same tone of voice back to her. Myra Barrs (1992: 20) writes about the importance of this echoing or 'shadowing' of the adult's voice: 'Mothers and teachers are often struck to hear their own intonational pattern being reproduced in children's independent reading. In reading with an adult, children can sometimes be observed to be "shadowing" the adult's voice.'

You will have to take it from me that this is what is happening in the reading of *Mr Gumpy's Outing*. We join the participants halfway through the story when the teacher is reading directly from the book. In the following text Anthony is joining in where he can, echoing his teacher's words. He already knows how the story goes and is able to anticipate a particular phrase, 'Can I come said the sheep', which he however reads as: 'Can I *go* said the sheep' (line 6).

But notice (line 7) that the teacher does not correct him at this point and instead she decides to carry on reading. She probably feels that a correction now would be inappropriate, perhaps because it would interrupt the flow of the story and perhaps also because she knows that the word 'come' is going to be repeated in a similar phrase later in the story, and Anthony will have an opportunity of hearing it again. And sure enough on line 12 Anthony hears his teacher read correctly 'can we *come* . . .'; on line 24 he volunteers 'Can I *come* said the . . .', showing that he has remembered the word 'come' and is using it correctly now. What we can't see also is that the teacher is pointing to 'come' as she reads, helping Anthony to make the connection between the written word and its sound:

1 *Teacher:* 'May I come please Mr Gum*py*?'
2 *Anthony:* -*py*
3 *Teacher:* 'said the –'
4 *Anthony:* the rabbit, the pig
5 *Teacher:* 'Very well but *don't* –'
6 *Anthony:* *don't* muck around. Can I go said the sheep?

In the following section (lines 7–11) Reid's question about the word 'bleating' indicates his growing interest in lexical knowledge. Notice how the teacher deals with his query. Even though there has been a misunderstanding, Reid is clearly paying attention to word meanings and his teacher will note this and talk about other word definitions if she has a chance:

7   *Teacher:* 'Yes, but don't keep bleating.'
8   *Reid:*   What's bleating mean?
9   *Teacher:* That's the sound the sheep make. When it goes baa-baa, we call that bleating.
10 *Reid:*   I thought you said bleeding.
11 *Teacher:* No. Bleating.

Following this explanatory conversation there is a discussion (lines 12–16) about whether a word should be read as 'chickens' or 'hens' (Reid says 'hens' and Anthony says 'chickens'). The teacher gently but firmly says that 'chickens' is the correct word and she points to it to reinforce the connection between the written word and its sound. It's noticeable that she chooses not to point out the initial digraph 'ch' here, though some teachers might have felt that this would reinforce the children's phonological knowledge. Perhaps she feels that a discussion about this consonant digraph would interrupt the momentum at this point and might have made too many demands on these young learners: a professional decision which only she is able to take at the time. She will no doubt make an opportunity to introduce the 'ch' digraph sooner or later, and when she does a reference back to the word 'chickens' in this book will certainly be appropriate.

12	*Teacher:*	'Can we come too said the –'
13	*Anthony:*	Two chickens
14	*Teacher:*	'Yes'
15	*Reid:*	Not chickens, hens
16	*Teacher:*	Well it says, it does say chickens. He was right.

Next (lines 17–21) we see the teacher allowing Anthony to make a judgement about what the chickens might do, and we know by her answer – 'I think they will' (line 21) – that she is listening carefully to what he says:

17	*Teacher:*	'Yes, but don't fl*ap*'
18	*Anthony:*	-*ap*
19	*Teacher:*	'said Mr –'
20	*Anthony:*	Gumpy. They will flap.
21	*Teacher:*	I think they will.

And then (lines 22–30) the teacher seizes the opportunity of giving the children some information about a specific word – 'calf', again encouraging the development of their lexical knowledge and taking this further by relating the word 'calf' to 'cow':

22	*Anthony:*	They will flap.
23	*Teacher:*	I think they will. 'Can –'
24	*Anthony:*	'Can I come said the –'
25	*Reid:*	cow
26	*Anthony:*	cow
27	*Teacher:*	Mmm. It's a baby one isn't it?
28	*Anthony:*	Yeah. It's growed up now.
29	*Teacher:*	Do you know what we call the baby one? Instead of calling it a cow we call it a calf don't we?
30	*Anthony:*	calf

Then (lines 31–3) Anthony increases his knowledge of syntax by repeating the phrase 'if you don't trample' after his teacher, luxuriating in the word 'trample' (line 32). His teacher notes later that she has never heard him say this word before; it's not part of his everyday vocabulary and she adds a comment to set the word 'trample' into its context to help Anthony understand what it means:

31 *Teacher:* 'Yes, if you don't trample'
32 *Anthony:* If you don't trample
33 *Teacher:* Mmm. He can go if he doesn't trample about.

The next part of the reading (lines 34–51) holds the anticipation and enjoyment of seeing each animal misbehave, with the inevitable consequences. The teacher encourages Anthony to take over the reading of key words at the end of each phrase, and she points to each word as he reads it to direct his gaze to it. Anthony knows what these animals do and this knowledge encourages him to insert the final words of each phrase into the space left by his teacher's anticipatory silence:

34 *Teacher:* 'For a little while they all went along happily but then the goat –'
35 *Anthony:* trampled
36 *Teacher:* He kicked. 'And the calf . . . *trampled*'
37 *Anthony:* *trampled*
38 *Teacher:* 'The chickens *flapped*'
39 *Anthony:* -apped
40 *Teacher:* 'The sheep bleated. The pig mucked a–'
41 *Anthony:* -bout
42 *Teacher:* 'The dog teased the –'
43 *Anthony:* cat
44 *Teacher:* 'The cat chased the –'
45 *Anthony:* rabbit
46 *Teacher:* 'The rabbit *hopped*'
47 *Anthony:* -opped
48 *Teacher:* 'The children *squabbled*'
49 *Anthony:* -abbled
50 *Teacher:* 'And into the water they all –'
51 *All:* fell

At this point (lines 52–63) Anthony and Reid begin a conversation about the story with their teacher and she makes a statement that takes them a little deeper into the text – 'I hope they can all swim' (line 55). This shows the boys that it is appropriate to pause and speculate about possible meanings; it also helps them to see that reading is sometimes about slowing down, savouring an event, thinking about the issues, allowing time to handle a complex area of knowledge. So the teacher shares her interest in the story and her concern for the characters by responding to the text alongside the children:

52   *Anthony:* Splash!
53   *Reid:*   Splash went the boat.
54   *Anthony:* It was a big boat that was. He shouldn't have let them in.
55   *Teacher:*   I hope they could all swim.
56   *Anthony:* I think so.
57   *Reid:*   The cat won't be able to.
58   *Teacher:*   Won't it?
59   *Reid:*   No.
60   *Anthony:* Cats can't swim.
61   *Teacher:*   Can't they? I don't think pigs can swim either.
62   *Anthony:* Pigs can't either.
63   *Teacher:*   Perhaps the water won't be too deep. Perhaps their feet will reach the bottom and they'll be able to walk.

And now Reid takes his contextual understanding further by exploring an event in his own life (lines 64–9). His teacher, far from seeing this as a diversion from the story, encourages him by asking questions. We already know that she is a good listener. Now, she helps Reid to add to his lexical knowledge by introducing the word 'shallow' and then demonstrating how 'deep' and 'shallow' can be paired together to describe the depth of the water. There can be no doubt of Reid's satisfaction in the telling of his tale:

64   *Reid:*   The other day I went I went to a swimming baths and I had a seat in a canoe boat with me and I went in a massive . . . I went in first the children's boat then mummy and daddy's boat and there was a deep end and a little end.
65   *Teacher:*   A deep end and a shallow end was it?
66   *Reid:*   And we taked the boat into the other one then I . . . went on my own.
67   *Teacher:*   Did you?
68   *Reid:*   But I had to have someone with me. That was my Liam.
69   *Teacher:*   And he helped look after you. Make sure you were safe . . . they needed someone to look after them, didn't they, in the story?

A great deal of energy has been expended in this reading of *Mr Gumpy's Outing*, but it has been worthwhile. The teacher has encouraged the children to respond to the story by discussing characters and events, and has handed over some of the reading to them, sensing that they had the confidence to have a go themselves. As well as being enjoyable in its own right, the session has enabled the teacher to familiarize herself with the children's level of knowledge and understanding. She knows now that they are aware of some of the language patterns in the text, and when she reads this story with them again she will help the boys to anticipate more key words and phrases in the text, building on their knowledge of written language and individual words. She has noted too that the boys have some bibliographic knowledge: they have some understanding that books are read from front to back, and that print is read from left to right and from top to bottom. She has observed too that the boys behave like readers because they listen and read with concentration – the reading session took 15 minutes altogether. She will use this knowledge to set up individual reading programmes for the children, and these will include rereading this and other texts, and introducing new ones that highlight particular kinds of reading knowledge she wants them to master.

Every reading encounter in this study is unique because people bring their own personalities, cultural knowledge and interests to the task and take from the experience their own particular thoughts and satisfactions; and if there is a close personal relationship between the adult and the child they are almost bound to communicate in ways that go beyond the information in the text. Taken as a whole, though, many of the story-reading sessions documented in this study share similar features that are particularly supportive to young children who are in the early stages of becoming readers. I have in mind especially those story-reading times where the teacher takes responsibility for ensuring that the child's fervent enjoyment and understanding of the story book remain a central purpose of the reading, alongside the introduction and encouragement of the study of language itself, its structure and grammar, and of individual words and the pattern of letters that make up those words. Victor Watson (1996b: 121) describes this teaching-and-learning model as being: 'community and conversation, a collaborative, reassuring and exploratory enterprise, which respects and empowers the sharing of meaning; a kind of talk, in fact'. The 'kind of talk' that Watson is highlighting is the sort that happens when the teacher makes comments that help the child build an image that holds the story together and gives it meaning –

exactly what is happening in the teaching session based on *Mr Gumpy's Outing*. While there can obviously be no set formula for this kind of encounter between an experienced reader, a child and a book in these early stages of learning to read, successful reading partnerships are likely to be those which are patterned in the way I have outlined here, closely controlled by an experienced reader who sets up and maintains the conditions for learning, and then trusts the child to learn.

The adult knows too that the child reader has a particular part to play in this kind of reading partnership. Young readers have to understand their role and their commitment to the task, since they are being asked to bring their own understanding to a book, actively, by working at the meaning. The children in this study who besieged tired adults with questions and comments about the book they were reading together, and who wanted to find out more about what was in the book by making connections with stories from their own lives, were positioning themselves within their own zone of proximal development and leaning on their adult guides for help in making sense of ideas. Often the child plays a part in negotiating reading time together. Reid often asks his teacher to read with him – and remember Gemma, who took a book home from school and pleaded with her mother to 'read it to me now' (p. 40). Time and again, the examples in this book have shown how important it is for the child to be willing to take on the role of the apprentice reader as described by Liz Waterland (1988), being prepared to join in, to ask questions, and to take over the physical task of holding the book and turning the pages. Indeed, the whole apprenticeship approach to reading is dependent on the child's willingness to cooperate. Indeed, without that willing engagement such collaboration is impossible. The child has to learn to take part in a conversation about a book, to bring thoughts and to share ideas from their own life, to trust the adult with those thoughts, to ask questions and to learn how to be a listener. The result is the kind of collaborative good practice demonstrated by the children and adults in Part 1 of this book.

And there is a third person involved in this transaction too; this is the author, who is obviously not physically present at the story reading but who is nevertheless represented through the words of the book, with the adult reader as mouthpiece. Authors become the sleeping partners in the reading encounter and have a subtle part to play in the child's reading experience through the impact of their books and the way in which they are written and designed to be read and shared. One of the tasks of the adult reader is to introduce the child and the author to each other.

Sometimes children can become each other's teachers, and though of course they are less experienced than adults in many ways, the young children in this study have shown that they are capable of sharing a book together from time to time and of learning from each other without adult intervention. Ellice Forman and Courtney Cazden's study of older children teaching younger ones (peer tutoring) and of children of the same age learning alongside each other (peer interaction) has shown that learning encounters between children without an adult present can be especially important because they form 'the only context in which children [can] reverse interactional roles with the same intellectual content, giving directions as well as following them, and asking questions as well as answering them' (1985: 344). The teaching and learning sessions between children in this study take place both at home and at school. Forman and Cazden, possibly with an eye on class sizes, point out that they 'may be especially important in school because of limitations and rigidities characteristic of adult–child interactions in that institutional setting' (1985: 344). Gemma and Geeta's retelling of the story of the three bears illustrates this kind of teaching and learning interaction well (p. 44–5). Their shared reading session began as a brief encounter with a well-loved story. During the time it took them to turn the pages, the two girls worked hard to retell the story in their own words – Geeta using her second language throughout – and in the end they brought it off well. We should applaud their single-mindedness and creativity, as they steadfastly clung to the task and took risks with each other's knowledge. There are countless examples of this kind of encounter happening in classrooms every day. They are dynamic and greatly enjoyed, and I cannot overemphasize the rewards – for both teachers and children – of setting up a classroom environment where the promise of taking hold of stories like this and learning to retell them to each other is supported by the teacher's invitation to 'go and read your book together'.

The central purpose of this chapter has been to show that adults who are aware of the ways they collaborate with their young readers help them to do something more difficult than they would be able to achieve on their own. They do this by being good reading models, by providing reading material sufficiently challenging to create and maintain interest and by encouraging a child to ask questions and make comments.

As long as experienced readers consciously and unconsciously act as reading models for children, young readers will learn from adults they wish to emulate. If they are invited to observe successful reading behaviour in teachers and other experienced readers at home, at school and in the wider community, they will want to become readers too. Children see the shape of their future reading biographies already written for them in the behaviour of older family members who unconsciously play out models of family uses of literacies; it is those home literacies and their link with the literacy practices of the school that I turn to now in the final chapter.

9

PATHWAYS TO

READING

Cocooned within the membership of a professional group in one culture and education system, it is easy to believe established theories and ideas to be 'natural' and unchangeable. Yet we do not have to travel far to realise that our beliefs on how children learn to read are determined by our own cultural group.

Eve Gregory (1996:10)

So far I have been concerned with describing and establishing what we can learn about young children's engagement with early literacy. I have explored the place of narrative in their lives and shown how their early reading experiences can be supported in partnership with a skilled reader. But I am conscious that in discussing the children's experiences and drawing generalizations from their early reading practices, my glimpse into their lives might unwittingly have implied that they share a common culture and a uniformity of reading experience. This was not my intention: a single cultural learning pattern cannot exist because the origins of the children's reading experiences lie in the social and cultural traditions of each of their families and are subject to their particular values and beliefs. Indeed, it is probably not even possible to make firm statements about the coherence of the home literacies for the two emergent bilingual children in this study, even though there might appear to be similarities between their linguistic and cultural practices.

All five children were already part of their own reading and writing networks before they started school, and their literacy learning had precise functions in each of their households. The print they saw around them at home gave them information about what people use written language for and their attitudes towards it. In the first part of this book the children's reading biographies document the creative and the passionate – as well as the more commonplace – kinds of reading and writing that formed part of their everyday lives: shopping lists and food labels, recipes, letter-reading, sending off for things, looking up information in books, checking on stolen car numbers, doing accounts and writing letters, as well as sharing the ritual of the bedtime story. Those who read sacred texts in their homes or at the temple were already part of a religious tradition with clear values and rules. And we have seen that the children had access to a wider network of media literacy, mainly through television and video programmes. In addition, nursery and playgroup experiences had given the children opportunities of using story in their play, trying out and extending the possibilities of their world, and of listening to stories. Even so, these experiences were not equally shared. Each child arrived at school with his or her own unique identity as a language user and with clear notions of the uses of literacy.

Sharing a book with a child is always a form of social interaction, involving a cultural transmission of attitudes, values, beliefs and skills. There is nothing 'natural' or indeed universal about any of the reading practices between parents, teachers and children that I have documented here. The idea of reading aloud to a child is not one that is practised in the home by all parents as a matter of course (Gemma's mother, remember, will only begin to read with her daughter when she comes to school; Geeta's parents are far too busy running their sewing factory to be able to read with their daughter). So reading with children at home is by no means a universal practice – and those adults who share a book with their child do so in remarkably different ways. Though Gemma's mother does what 'comes naturally' when she reads with her daughter (p. 43), she is in fact applying her own cultural knowledge of being a mother to the way she conducts the reading sessions. Marilyn Cochran-Smith reminds us that:

> Children . . . are not born knowing how to connect their knowledge and experience in 'literate' ways to printed and pictorial texts. Rather, they must learn strategies for understanding texts just as they must learn the ways of eating and talking that are appropriate to their cultures or social groups.
>
> (Cochran-Smith 1986: 36)

The picture books on the shelves in the children's classrooms do not come free of this cultural fashioning. There are underlying cultural assumptions and expectations behind their construction, and they presuppose a particular way of reading by an adult and an apprentice child reader. Their words, design and illustrations are fashioned to enable young children and their teachers to talk about the meaning of a story in a conversational style and to foster imaginative insights. Some books invite their readers to repeat a formula over and over again (think of 'and he went rumpeta, rumpeta, rumpeta all the way down the road', from *The Elephant and the Bad Baby* (Vipont 1969)). Others encourage the shared expression of laughter at awkward situations (think of what happens to the fox in *Rosie's Walk* (Hutchins 1968)), or help children to make connections with similar stories (think of all the well-known stories embedded in *The Jolly Postman* (Ahlberg and Ahlberg 1986) or *Each Peach Pear Plum* (Ahlberg and Ahlberg 1978)). Authors who write books like these give particular value to the specific cultural frameworks that help them to form and express their thought and creativity, and as a result they produce their works with a particular audience in mind – notably the child reader who is socialized into transferring the pictures and the print into a celebratory and often impassioned conversation, asking questions about the story, proposing what might happen next and checking this information against experiences in their own lives. The books become a powerful source of creativity, requiring children to investigate and use their imaginations, to stop and discuss and to interpret the words of the author. Cochran-Smith has pointed out that 'the texts and designs of picture books for young children assume, and are directly related to, the adult child oral language patterns of the social groups that produce and use them' (1986: 41). This presupposes a particular way of reading – a system of understanding – that may not be shared by some families. Tensions can be set up between child, teacher and parent if there is a cultural mismatch about the way a book is to be read and understood by a child. Eve Gregory, in her work with emergent bilingual readers, says significantly:

> We cannot assume that the rules and recipes of the British school are superior to those in any other culture in which children are successfully learning to read . . . We cannot assume that teachers, children and their families enter school with the same 'sense' of reading. Recognising the wealth of knowledge and reading practices brought by children from

home at the same time as introducing them explicitly to our cultural rules will be important first steps towards enabling children to 'situate' themselves in the social context of reading in the classroom.

(Gregory 1996: 45)

Reid's parents regularly read bedtime stories with him, and it comes as no surprise that they were both read to themselves as children, and place a high value on the enjoyment of stories. They have remained readers all their lives and so, though they may not realize it, reading aloud to Reid is a cultural practice influenced by their own literacy history. So, too, is the way they share a book with their son. He is included in conversations and decision-making at home about all kinds of issues that relate to the family, and this interaction is evident in the story-reading session with his mother (p. 88–91). In contrast, Gurdeep's reading time with his father is of a totally different order, with no direct invitation for Gurdeep to negotiate the text through conversation (p. 30–2). Neither of Gurdeep's parents was brought up in a cultural or educational tradition where picture books were used to teach early reading, and his father has to make adjustments to his concept of what reading a book with his son means as he reads Gurdeep a bedtime story. Eve Gregory reminds us that for some families: 'the use of story books for beginning reading may not correspond to [their] interpretation of what "counts" as valid material for learning to read' (1996: 83). Her words are a timely reminder that it is necessary now for teachers to acknowledge what counts as 'valid' in children's lives outside school. As I write I have in front of me two books given to me by 10-year-old Mohammed, who used to read to me at school. Both books are slim volumes, about 4 inches by 7 inches, surprisingly light to pick up, with a red patterned cover of stiff card and soft flimsy paper inside. Arabic texts from the Qur'an fill the pages of one book. There are of course no pictures. The borders are highly decorated with elegant symmetrical patterns. The other book has rows of separate characters, about 50 on each page. It appears to be an exercise book of some kind. These books formed part of Mohammed's religious literacy programme at the temple and he seemed to enjoy reading them to me, rocking gently backwards and forwards in a kind of rhythmic and spiritual contemplation.

For each child in this study the school is the common cultural link, the base from which they will do a great deal of reading and writing, some of which is shared with their parents. To help them and other children like them to become literate in the fullest sense, we need now to set up total literacy environments for them, ones that embrace the views of parents, teachers and children, ones that encompass learning in the home and the community – including community language schools, as well as in the classroom. As I reflect on the bedtime-reading session where Gurdeep insisted on seeing the picture of the snake again, to the consternation of his father (p. 31) I recall Eve Gregory's observation of the difficulty facing parents who have 'no real idea' about how reading is taught in school and for whom 'expectations of their own role in the process [are not] made explicit' by the primary school. Gregory also observed that parents of emergent bilingual readers in her study were 'waiting for homework where they [could] help their children step-by-step' and that usually the reading books their children brought home from school were 'too hard, contain[ed] no direct instructions, and [left] them floundering' (1996: 44).

As a head teacher, in the days before I undertook this study, I believed that it would be a simple matter to involve parents in helping their children to read at home, and the staff and I embarked on a series of parents' workshops about the teaching and learning of reading. We also wrote a booklet containing advice for parents. I have written elsewhere (Minns 1993b) of the difficulties involved in trying to write such a booklet for an audience of parents from different cultural traditions, because of the problems of trying to embrace their various linguistic and cultural expectations. The problems raised by the writing of this booklet manifested themselves in some of the statements it contained. For example, when I wrote 'What we would like is for you to read the story to your child', I had certainly not taken into account the different ways that parents read with their children at home. I did not know then that some parents preferred to read the book first and then invite their child to read to them, or that others might feel constrained when their child interjected and broke the flow of the text. My advice to 'choose a quiet time when you can read together' and to 'spend as much time together as you can', took no account of some family commitments that meant parents had very little time in which to 'choose' to read. My well-intentioned observation that it was 'important for children to see their parents reading and getting information from books' might have been of some value to Reid's father, who spent time researching insects, or even perhaps to Geeta's father who used the Yellow Pages frequently – and they could give themselves a pat on the back for doing what the school considered to be good practice. But I took no account of the parents for whom 'getting information and enjoyment' from books was not culturally significant.

It is probably becoming clear that the school had, with the best of intentions, set itself the task of directing the reading behaviours of families from diverse communities within the school catchment area, without taking any notice of their differing individual and cultural needs. The use of the word 'we' to indicate the views of the school ('we' appears over and over again in the booklet) shows clear ownership of knowledge and of the form in which it is to be transferred from school to home. It is profoundly unhelpful to say that I knew no better, but I really did not. To say to parents: 'Make sure there are children's books in the home. Use the local library and if you want to buy books, get advice from the school and choose wisely' might have appealed to Reid and Gurdeep's parents (though they needed no advice on what to choose); I can only think that Gemma's parents might have ignored a piece of 'advice' that probably made little sense to them and that cut across their established literacy behaviour. It is also significant that I addressed the booklet to *parents*, because I knew nothing then of the vital support that older brothers and sisters like Ranu and Tejinder often give, both as reading models and as sharers of books. Some years later I wrote:

> Well-meaning advice such as this was based on my profes-
> sional knowledge of how young children come to view the
> task of learning to read, and I will still argue that parents who
> support their young child in a way which is patient and lov-
> ing, and show a genuine interest in both the text and the
> child learner, will be setting firm foundations for the child's
> reading life. But it is important to remind myself that this
> belief is borne out of my own cultural experience as a reader
> and as a teacher, and that Mohammed, who learns to read
> the Qur'an at the temple, does so largely by rote-learning the
> written symbols; a smack across the head is the penalty for a
> badly-learnt lesson. He is accepting of this . . . The advice I
> gave might have been useful to those whose lifestyle fol-
> lowed the mainstream culture of the school closely; I suspect
> that for many parents what I wrote was so alien to their way
> of living that they simply ignored it.
>
> (Minns 1993b: 29)

I hope I know better now. After all, my booklet was written over a decade ago. How much more sound is the current literature that shows parents and teachers working together to produce reading advice for their school communities. I have in mind those booklets written with the support of the City Lit project. One begins:

> As parents and teachers we feel that all children are special and we need to work together to give each child the best start in education that we can. Because reading is such an important part of education and children need to share books and read as much as possible, we thought a book written BY PARENTS FOR PARENTS would be a great help. As parents, we don't all find reading so easy. In fact, many of us find it quite difficult but we still want to help our children. Please feel you can ask for help from the school. This is NOT a book of rules. Please use the ideas in it to suit you and your children.
>
> (Stoker *et al*. c. 1992: 1)

Another begins:

> As parents we have taught our children so much before they even get to school to start their formal education. But once they start school parents are not always sure how best to help. Schools welcome parents' involvement and know it is important in helping children do well. This booklet has been written by a group of parents. It tries to cover some of the questions parents ask about helping their children to read and gives some tips and ideas about how to make reading more enjoyable. All our children are special and unique and they learn to read in different ways and at different speeds. Anything we can do to encourage them to read will be a help.
>
> (Stoker *et al*. c. 1993: 1)

These booklets are impressive because they reflect the actual voices of the parents in the school community where they are produced and used. The parents become the 'we' of the text. These schools have set up a dialogue with parents about the teaching and learning of reading – a dialogue that reflects a variety of practices at home and at school, with a clear framework of ideas and suggestions, ranging from choosing and sharing books to reading public print. When schools can be encouraged to set up strong community links with parents, teachers are in a much better position to learn about children's early literacies in the home and to include parents in assessment and record-keeping practices. This enables teachers and parents to share knowledge about crucial areas of learning, including the language or languages in which that learning happens. Individual meetings with parents of pre-school children help teachers to find out about this range of learning in the early years and to consider the most appropriate ways of teaching young children to read and write. A set of questions for parents might look something like this, though they would obviously need adapting to meet the needs of particular schools and communities:

Introductory and background
- What were the first words your child said?
- When your child began to walk and talk, what kinds of things did he or she begin to show an interest in?

Language
- What is your child's first language? Does he or she know and use any other languages?
- What languages do you and other family members speak?

Play
- What were your child's first toys?
- What kinds of things does your child like playing?
- Has your child been to nursery or playgroup?
- Has pre-school experience helped your child?

Reading, writing and storytelling
- What sort of things does your child read/write/draw?
- Does your child have his or her own books? If so, what are they? Who chooses them?
- Do you or your child belong to a library?
- Does your child read anything when you are outside (e.g. food labels in shops, street names, bus numbers)?
- Does anyone in your house read to your child?
- Does anyone tell your child stories? If so, who? And when? Does your child enjoy listening to stories?
- Does your child have a favourite story?
- Does your child tell you stories?
- Does your child hear or tell jokes, rhymes, songs, etc.?
- Has your child ever worked with a computer?
- Does your child watch TV? If so, what programmes/adverts are favourites?
- How important is reading and writing to you?

- Do you read/write? If so, what? Does your child see you reading/writing?
- Did your parents or grandparents read? Did your parents tell you stories?
- What were your own early experiences of learning to read and write (a) at home (b) at school?

Planning for school
- What were your own early experiences of school?
- Do you think your child's experiences of school will be like your own?

When parents are given the opportunity to answer questions and talk about their own children, making a narrative of their early experiences, it becomes clear that they are careful observers of their own child's learning and growth. It is worth recalling some of the parents' careful observations of their child's early learning in this study:

of Gurdeep:

> When he was a baby you'd be reading or writing and he'd be out there sitting in that corner and quickly he would pick it up (p. 22).

> Gurdeep sits with me and he wants to touch [the holy book]. I tell him the words are in Punjabi (p. 26).

of Gemma:

> I used to sit at one end and her dad used to sit a bit nearer and I used to say, 'come on', and we used to do it for hours. She wasn't long walking (p. 44).

> We'd say everything we'd seen, like. I think 'dog' was quite a quick word with her because she liked dogs. Then 'nan' and 'grandad'. She seemed to pick them up. She more or less learned herself (p. 44).

> When you're reading her stories she takes it all in. 'Cos if I read the book over again to her she's telling me what's coming on the page. In one book she says, 'and he told her off' and before I turn the page over she knew it was on the next page (p. 43).

of Anthony:

> I just let it come on its own 'cos it's better that way. They sort
> of pick up things here and there. If you push them too much
> it takes longer. They lose interest in what you're trying to tell
> them (p. 56–7).

> We go back through the book and I say to him, 'What's hap-
> pening there?' then he can tell me everything that's happen-
> ing, before it's happened . . . you just can't read to him. You've
> got to hold the book so he can see the pictures . . . (p. 56).

of Geeta:

> She doesn't know the ABC but she still brings a book . . . [She]
> tries to read according to the pictures (p. 69).

And the parents of course, have expectations for their children, and want them to do well at school:

of Gemma:

> I'd like Gemma to get something, not just go into a factory
> like I did (p. 36)

> We'll have to get some more decent books. I'll be reading
> with her now she's starting school. Now she's old enough to
> appreciate it (p. 37).

of Anthony:

> I think school will change him a lot (p. 55).

of Reid:

> We look for the learning potential in everything. We believe
> in spending time constructively and creatively as a way of
> preparing the children for life (p. 84).

These views about learning have grown from family patterns
that seek to develop a satisfactory – and satisfying – life plan for
each child. They form part of a set of beliefs about living and learning that have developed within each family and have often been
remembered from the parents' own childhood and school days. As
the parents emphasize the importance of their child's learning

they also increasingly give themselves a role as observers and teachers, and their insights into their child's learning patterns, their awareness of the child's needs, come over in their enthusiastic and passionate observations.

The use of the *Primary Language Record* in schools (Barrs *et al.* 1988) has done a great deal to add a social dimension to our knowledge of the literacy process, helping teachers explore new ways of looking at what children are learning both at home and at school. The *Primary Language Record* advocates the use of parent conferences, and shows how parents' comments can be carefully recorded, giving opportunities for teachers and parents to discuss each child's views and experiences of reading and writing. Conferences like these provide teachers with opportunities for learning more about a child's progress and about what parents might have already done to help their children learn to read. Teachers and parents who set up a two-way flow of information, with teachers sharing their more developed expertise with parents, and parents sharing with teachers their knowledge about the kinds of literacies they offer children, including ways of sharing books, will be working together to help children make the most of their school experience.

Exciting home–school projects are running in various local authorities that encourage parents to work alongside their children at home and at school in a variety of imaginative ways, and their use gives parents back the sense of power they might have lost when they read my original reading booklet. For example:

- parents working with computers and using CD-ROMs in the classroom to extend their child's knowledge of stories;
- parents videoing their own child taking part in reading activities at regular intervals through the school year, and discussing the child's progress with the teacher;
- workshop sessions where parents can work alongside each other to exchange views on how they encourage their children to read and write at home;
- bilingual parents tape-recording stories from their own culture for children to listen to in school;
- parents sitting with children in the classroom to hear stories told or read by the teacher, then rereading or retelling the stories at home with their child.

When the five children in this study arrived at school they each brought with them distinct views of reading and writing which came up against the school view in a new social environment. Schools in general are perhaps still not as aware as they should be of early home experiences of literacy. In order to become con- scious of pre-school experiences and their differences and to add a social dimension to our knowledge of the reading process, it is time now to give ourselves a new way of looking at what children might be doing when they come to school at the age of 4. At present, in spite of the projects I have mentioned above, and the use of the *Primary Language Record* in areas around the country, we still know too little about the knowledge of reading that children bring to school with them, and still less about what their parents might have done to help children learn to read – in spite of their involve- ment with home–school reading programmes. Our knowledge of the cultural beliefs and values of families and their effect on chil- dren has to be made a professional concern. Specifically we need a detailed knowledge of the kinds of literacies available to a child and the ways the child is socialized into responding, including ways of sharing books. Only by acquiring this kind of knowledge will we know how a child views the task of learning to read when he or she enters school.

Children become part of a new social group when they come to school and bring with them views of themselves as learners. It is crucial that the school helps them to build on that view by showing children that their pre-school experience is valid and significant, and finding ways of reflecting it back to them. Teachers can no longer think in terms of a single standardized schooled literacy which functions irrespective of the child's background. There must be acknowledgement that the experience of literacy is inseparable from the experience of family life. Children take reading experi- ences from school to home for their parents to share; it is therefore important that the school's view of literacy is made explicit for parents, so that both they and teachers can work together in full knowledge of what the other is doing. It is too easy for the school to diminish the child as a learner by ignoring, or having no knowl- edge of, previously acquired competences.

I began work on this study some ten years ago in order to find out more about the processes of learning to read at home and at school. My brief glimpse into the reading lives and literacies of Gemma, Gurdeep, Anthony, Reid and Geeta has enabled me to see that any reading a child encounters in school always has a previous history. The children did not arrive at school illiterate: each one of them brought with them to school their own unique reading experiences, learned socially in their family and community. I have tried to make these explicit through the children's reading biographies and the discussions which followed.

Nearly 30 years ago James Britton wrote:

> in school we cannot afford to ignore all that has gone on before. So often in the past we have tried to make a fresh start, at the risk of cutting off the roots which alone can sustain the growth we look for. It is not only that the classroom must more and more merge into the world outside it, but that the processes of school learning must merge into the processes of learning that begin at birth and are life-long. We can no longer regard school learning as simply an interim phase, a period of instruction and apprenticeship that marks the change from immaturity to maturity, from play in the nursery to work in the world. School learning must both build upon the learning of infancy and foster something that will continue and evolve through adult life.
>
> (Britton 1970: 129)

If anything, these words have even greater significance today than they had in the 1970s. For Gemma, Gurdeep, Geeta, Reid, Anthony and countless other children, learning to read will continue and evolve through adult life if the processes of learning in school and in the community can keep in touch with each other.

REFERENCES AND FURTHER READING

Children's books and reading schemes

Ahlberg, A. and Ahlberg, J. (1977) *Burglar Bill*. London: Picture Lions.
Ahlberg, A. and Ahlberg, J. (1978) *Each Peach Pear Plum*. London: Kestrel Books.
Ahlberg, A. and Ahlberg, J. (1986) *The Jolly Postman or Other People's Letters*. London: Heinemann.
Briggs, R. (1978) *The Snowman*. London: Hamish Hamilton.
Britton, J. and Root, B. (advisers) (1978) *Reading 360: The Ginn Reading Programme*. Aylesbury: Ginn.
Browne, A. (1983) *Gorilla*. London: Magnet.
Burningham, J. (1970) *Mr Gumpy's Outing*. London: Cape.
Burningham, J. (1984) *Granpa*. London: Cape.
Carle, E. (1970) *The Very Hungry Caterpillar*. London: Hamish Hamilton.
Eastman, P. D. (1960) *Are You My Mother?* London: Collins.
Evans, E. (1985) *That Fat Cat*. London: Circle Books.
Frith, M. (1973) *I'll Teach My Dog 100 Words*. London: Collins.
Furchgott, T. (1983) *Nanda in India*. London: Deutsch.
Hill, E. (1984) *Good Morning Baby Bear*. London: Heinemann.
Hill, P. (1980) *The Noisiest Class in School*. Leamington Spa: Scholastic.
Hughes, S. (1977) *Dogger*. London: The Bodley Head.
Hutchins, P. (1968) *Rosie's Walk*. London: The Bodley Head.
Jackson, M. (1988) *Moonwalker*. London: Heinemann.
McKee, D. (1980) *Not Now Bernard*. London: Andersen Press.
Milligan, S. (1968) *Silly Verse for Kids*. Harmondsworth: Puffin

Murray, W. (1964) *The Ladybird Key Words Reading Scheme*. Loughborough: Wills and Hepworth.

Nicoll, H. and Pienkowski, J. (1972) *Meg and Mog*. Harmondsworth: Puffin.

O'Donnell, M. and Munro, R. (1966) *Kathy and Mark Basic Readers*. Welwyn: James Nisbet.

O'Donnell, M., Munro, R. and Warwick, M. (1949) *Janet and John*. Welwyn: James Nisbet.

Rosen, M. (1981) *You Can't Catch Me*. London: Deutsch.

Rosen, M. (1989) *We're Going on a Bear Hunt*. London: Walker Books.

Schonell, F. and Serjeant, I. (1958) *The Happy Venture Readers*. Edinburgh: Oliver and Boyd.

Sendak, M. (1970) *Where the Wild Things Are*. Harmondsworth: Puffin.

Smith, D. (1956) *One Hundred and One Dalmatians*. London: Heinemann.

Smith, W. J. (1981) The Toaster, in J. Bennett (ed.) *Tiny Tim, Verses for Children*. London: Heinemann.

Southgate, V. (1971) *Goldilocks and the Three Bears*. Loughborough: Ladybird Books.

Southgate, V. (1972) *Little Red Riding Hood*. Loughborough: Ladybird Books.

Stone, S. (1985) *The Naughty Mouse*. London: Luzac Storytellers.

Tomlinson, J. (1968) *The Owl who was Afraid of the Dark*. Harmondsworth: Puffin.

Vipont, E. (1969) *The Elephant and the Bad Baby*. London: Hamish Hamilton.

Wagner, J. (1977) *John Brown, Rose and the Midnight Cat*. London: Viking Kestrel.

Walker, B. K. (1975) *Teeny Tiny and the Witch Woman*. Harmondsworth: Puffin.

Wolff, M. (1979) *Me in Puddles*. London: Abelard.

Worthington, P. and Worthington, S. (1981) *Teddy Bear Postman*. Harmondsworth: Puffin.

Academic books and journal articles

Ashton-Warner, S. (1963) *Teacher*. London: Secker and Warburg.

Barrs, M. (1992) The tune on the page, in K. Kimberley, M. Meek and J. Miller (eds) *New Readings: Contributions to an Understanding of Literacy*. London: A. and C. Black, 16–28.

Barrs, M. and Thomas, A. (eds) (1991) *The Reading Book*. London: Centre for Language in Primary Education.

Barrs, M., Ellis, S., Hester, H. and Thomas, A. (1988) *The Primary Language Record Handbook*. London: Centre for Language in Primary Education.

Bennett, J. (1979) *Learning to Read with Picture Books*. Stroud: Thimble Press.

Bernstein, B. (1970) A critique of the concept of 'compensatory education', in D. Rubinstein and C. Stoneman (eds) *Education for Democracy*. Harmondsworth: Penguin, 110–21.

Brice Heath, S. (1983) *Ways with Words: Language, Life and Work in Communities and Classrooms*. Cambridge: Cambridge University Press.

Britton, J. (1970) *Language and Learning*. Harmondsworth: Penguin.

Bruner, J. (1986) *Actual Minds, Possible Words.* Cambridge, MA: Harvard University Press.

Bussis, A., Chittenden, E., Amerel, M. and Klausner, E. (1985) *Inquiry into Meaning: An Investigation of Learning to Read.* Hillsdale, NJ: Lawrence Erlbaum.

Clark, M. M. (1994) *Young Literacy Learners: How We Can Help Them.* Leamington Spa: Scholastic.

Cochran-Smith, M. (1986) Reading to children: a model for understanding texts, in B. B. Schieffelin and P. Gilmore (eds) *The Acquisition of Literacy: Ethnographic Perspectives.* Norwood, NJ: Ablex, 35–54.

Crystal, D. (1987) *The Cambridge Encyclopaedia of Language.* Cambridge: Cambridge University Press.

Department for Education (1995) *Key Stages 1 and 2 of the National Curriculum.* London: HMSO.

Department of Education and Science and the Welsh Office (1989) *English in the National Curriculum.* London: HMSO.

Dombey, H. (1992) *Words and Worlds: Reading in the Early Years of School.* Sheffield: National Association for the Teaching of English and National Association of Advisers in English.

Doonan, J. (1993) *Looking at Pictures in Picture Books.* Stroud: Thimble Press.

Eliot, G. (1977) Janet's Repentance, in *Scenes of Clerical Life.* Harmondsworth, Penguin [first published in 1858].

Forman, E. A. and Cazden, C. B. (1985) Exploring Vygotskian perspectives in education: the cognitive value of peer interaction, in J. V. Wertsch (ed.) *Culture, Communication and Cognition: Vygotskian Perspectives.* Cambridge: Cambridge University Press.

Fox, C. (1983) *At the Very Edge of the Forest: The Influence of Literature on Storytelling by Children.* London: Cassell.

Fox, C. (1989) Children thinking through story, *English in Education,* 23(2): 25–36.

Graham, J. (1990) *Pictures on the Page.* Sheffield: National Association for the Teaching of English.

Gregory, E. (1996) *Making Sense of a New World: Learning to Read in a Second Language.* London: Paul Chapman.

Harding, D. W. (1967) Considered experience: the invitation of the novel, *English in Education,* 1(2): 7–15.

Hardy, B. (1977) Narrative as a primary act of mind, in M. Meek, A. Warlow and G. Barton (eds) *The Cool Web: The Pattern of Children's Reading.* London: The Bodley Head, 12–23.

Iser, W. (1978) *The Act of Reading: A Theory of Aesthetic Response.* London: Routledge and Kegan Paul.

Jackson, B. (1979) *Starting School.* London: Croom Helm.

Ketch, A. (1991) The delicious alphabet, *English in Education,* 25(1): 1–4.

Kimberley, K., Meek, M. and Miller, J. (eds) (1992) *New Readings: Contributions to an Understanding of Literacy.* London: A. and C. Black.

Maharaj Charan Singh (1966) *The Master Answers.* Punkab: India.

Meek, M. (1982) *Learning to Read*. London: The Bodley Head.

Meek, M. (1991) *On Being Literate*. London: The Bodley Head.

Meek, M., Warlow, A. and Barton, G. (eds) (1977) *The Cool Web: The Pattern of Children's Reading*. London: The Bodley Head.

Minns, H. (1993a) Three ten year old boys and their reading, in M. Barrs and S. Pidgeon (eds) *Reading the Difference: Gender and Reading in the Primary School*. London: Centre for Language in Primary Education.

Minns, H. (1993b) 'Don't tell them Daddy taught you': the place of parents or putting parents in their place, in M. Styles and M. J. Drummond (eds) *The Politics of Reading*. Cambridge: University of Cambridge and Homerton College, 25–32.

Rosen, H. (c. 1984) *Stories and Meanings*. Sheffield: National Association for the Teaching of English.

Schieffelin, B. B. and Gilmore, P. (eds) (1986) *The Acquisition of Literacy: Ethnographic Perspectives*. Norwood, NJ: Ablex.

Scholes, P. (1991) *The Oxford Companion to Music*. Oxford: Oxford University Press [first published in 1938].

Smith, F. (1971) *Understanding Reading*. New York: Holt, Rinehart and Winston.

Smith, F. (1973) *Psycholinguistics and Reading*. New York: Holt, Rinehart and Winston.

Smith, F. (1978) *Reading*. Cambridge: Cambridge University Press.

Smith, F. (1984) *Essays into Literacy: Selected Papers and Some Afterthoughts*. Portsmouth, NH: Heinemann.

Spencer, M. (1976) Stories are for telling, *English in Education*, 10(1): 16–23.

Steedman, C. (1992) *Amarjit's Song in Past Tenses: Essays on Writing, Autobiography and History*. London: Rivers Oram.

Steedman, C., Urwin, C. and Walkerdine, V. (eds) (1985) *Language, Gender and Childhood*. London: Routledge and Kegan Paul.

Stoker, D., Nys, L. and parents of Eveline Lowe School, Southwark, London (c. 1992) *The 'Good Time' Reading Guide*. London: Southwark Education Department and The City Lit.

Stoker, D. and parents of Bessemer Grange Infant School, Southwark, London (c. 1993) *Parents to Parents: Helping Our Children to Read*. London: Southwark Education Department and The City Lit.

Tansley, A. E. (1967) *Reading and Remedial Reading*. London: Routledge and Kegan Paul.

Taylor, D. (1983) *Family Literacy: Young Children Learning to Read and Write*. Exeter: NH: Heinemann.

Vygotsky, L. S. (1978) *Mind in Society: The Development of Higher Psychological Processes*. Cambridge, MA: Harvard University Press.

Wade, B. (1982) Reading rickets and the uses of story, *English in Education*, 16(3): 28–37.

Walker, A. (1983) *The Color Purple*. London: The Women's Press.

Waterland, L. (1988) *Read with Me: An Apprenticeship Approach to Reading*. Stroud: Thimble Press.

Watson, V. (1996a) The left-handed reader – linear sentences and unmapped pictures, in V. Watson and M. Styles (eds) *Talking Pictures: Pictorial Texts and Young Readers.* London: Hodder and Stoughton, 145–63.

Watson, V. (1996b) Her family's voices – one young reader tuning into reading, in V. Watson and M. Styles (eds) *Talking Pictures: Pictorial Texts and Young Readers.* London: Hodder and Stoughton, 112–22.

Watson, V. and Styles, M. (1996) *Talking Pictures: Pictorial Texts and Young Readers.* London: Hodder and Stoughton.

Weir, R. (1970) *Language in the Crib.* The Hague: Mouton.

Wells, G. (1981) *Learning Through Interaction.* Cambridge: Cambridge University Press.

Wells, G. (1985) *Language, Learning and Education.* London: NFER-Nelson.

Wells, G. (1987) *The Meaning Makers.* London: Hodder and Stoughton.

Wertsch, J. V. (ed.) (1985) *Culture, Communication and Cognition: Vygotskian Perspectives.* Cambridge: Cambridge University Press.

Whitehead, M. (1990) *Language and Literacy in the Early Years.* London: Paul Chapman.

Widlake, P. and Macleod, F. (1984) *Raising Standards.* Coventry: Community Education Development Centre.

Further reading

Adams, M. J. (1990) *Beginning to Read: Thinking and Learning about Print.* Cambridge, MA: MIT Press.

Applebee, A. N. (1978) *The Child's Concept of Story.* Chicago: University of Chicago Press.

Bettelheim, B. (1978) *The Uses of Enchantment.* Harmondsworth: Penguin.

Bloom, W. (1987) *Partnership with Parents in Reading.* London: Hodder and Stoughton.

Britton, J. (1987) Vygotsky's contribution to pedagogical theory, *English in Education,* 21(3): 22–6.

Clark, M. M. (1976) *Young Fluent Readers.* London: Heinemann.

Cook, E. (1969) *The Ordinary and the Fabulous.* Cambridge: Cambridge University Press.

Cook-Gumperz, J. (ed.) (1986) *The Social Construction of Literacy.* Cambridge: Cambridge University Press.

Fry, D. (1985) *Children Talk about Books: Seeing Themselves as Readers.* Milton Keynes: Open University Press.

Goelman, H., Oberg, A. and Smith, F. (eds) (1984) *Awakening to Literacy.* Exeter: Heinemann Educational.

Gollasch, F. (ed.) (1972) *Language and Literacy: The Collected Writings of Kenneth S. Goodman.* London: Routledge and Kegan Paul.

Levine, K. (1986) *The Social Context of Literacy.* London: Routledge and Kegan Paul.

Meek, M. (ed.) (1983) *Opening Moves: Work in Progress in the Study of Children's Language Development*. London: Institute of Education, University of London.

Meek, M. (1988) *How Texts Teach What Children Learn*. Stroud: Thimble Press.

Meek, M. and Mills, C. (eds) (1988) *Language and Literacy in the Primary School*. London: Falmer.

Miller, J. (ed.) (1982) *Eccentric Propositions: Essays on Literature and the Curriculum*. London: Routledge and Kegan Paul.

Minns, H. (1987) 'From home to school: learning to read', MA thesis. Institute of Education, University of London.

Minns, H. (1990) *Read It To Me Now! Learning to Read at Home and at School*. London: Virago.

Moon, C. (ed.) (1985) *Practical Ways to Teach Reading*. London: Ward Lock.

O'Sullivan, O. (1995) *The Primary Language Record in Use*. London: Centre for Language in Primary Education.

Rubinstein, D. and Stoneman, C. (eds) (1970) *Education for Democracy*. Harmondsworth: Penguin.

Street, B. V. (1984) *Literacy in Theory and Practice*. Cambridge: Cambridge University Press.

Styles, M. and Drummond, M. J. (eds) (1993) *The Politics of Reading*. Cambridge: University of Cambridge and Homerton College.

INDEX

TOWARDS READING
LITERACY DEVELOPMENT IN THE PRE-SCHOOL YEARS

Linda Miller

* How can teachers, nursery nurses and child-care workers ensure that pre-school children develop essential literacy skills?
* What role can parents play?
* Can children's home experiences be built upon in the classroom or nursery?

This book brings together recent research on early literacy development and presents it accessibly to answer these and other questions. All aspects of early literacy development are considered – the development of skills necessary for later success in reading and writing, including the importance of rhyme and environmental print.

A theme which runs throughout the book is that parents and professional educators need to work in partnership. Linda Miller describes a range of recent projects which have involved parents in their young children's literacy development and offers practical suggestions for implementing such projects. Strategies for observing, recording and providing for young children's literacy developments in a wide range of pre-school and early years settings are also discussed.

The book will be valuable reading for anyone working with young children in pre-school and early years settings and will also be of great interest to parents.

Contents
Introduction – The emergence of literacy – Towards reading: what children come to know – Towards writing: what children come to know – The role of parents in literacy development – Family literacy – Sharing books in the pre-school: what children learn – Parents as partners: setting up a literacy project – Observing and recording early literacy development – Provision for literacy in the pre-school – The supporting adult – Continuity between home and pre-school – References – Index.

144pp   0 335 19212 7 (Paperback)   0 335 19216 5 (Hardback)

READING IN THE EARLY YEARS HANDBOOK

Robin Campbell

Reading in the Early Years Handbook is a reference text covering all aspects of young children learning to read. It deals with a comprehensive list of topics ranging from *apprenticeship approach* to *nursery rhymes* to *whole language*. The text also deals with organizational issues such as *classroom management* and *time for literacy*. In all, some 60 topics are presented alphabetically and each of these topics is followed by suggestions for further reading. Additionally, several topics have 'In the classroom' sections where examples from the classroom are used to highlight the particular issues. The comprehensive material is presented in a handbook format to enable easy access for readers.

Contents
Introduction – Apprenticeship approach – Assessment – Audience – Big books – Breakthrough to literacy – Bullock Report – Classroom management – Classroom organization – Classroom print – Computers – Conferencing – Cue systems – Discussions – Emerging literacy – Environmental print – Formula for beginning reading – Genres – Hearing children read – Home-school links – Illustrations – Invented spelling – Knowledge about language – Language experience approach – Left-to-right directionality – Library corner – Listening area – Methods – Miscue analysis – National curriculum – Nursery rhymes – Organic vocabulary – Paired reading – Phonemic awareness – Phonics teaching – Play activities – Punctuation – Reading drive – Reading non-fiction – Reading recovery – Reading schemes – Real books – Real books approach – Record-keeping – Responding to miscues – Running records – Scanning and skimming – School policy – Shared reading – Standard Assessment Tasks – Story grammar – Story readings – Sustained silent reading – Teacher's role – Text-to-life connections – Thematic work/topic work – Time for literacy – Whole language – Writing – Writing centre – Your classroom – References.

192pp   0 335 19309 9 (Paperback)   0 335 19310 2 (Hardback)